Not Too Sweet

ALSO BY JESSICA SEINFELD

*Vegan, at Times: 120 Recipes for Every Day
or Every So Often*

*Food Swings: 125+ Recipes to Enjoy Your
Life of Virtue and Vice*

*The Can't Cook Book: 100+ Recipes for
the Absolutely Terrified!*

*Double Delicious!: Good, Simple Food for
Busy, Complicated Lives*

*Deceptively Delicious: Simple Secrets to
Get Your Kids Eating Good Food*

Not Too Sweet

100 Dessert Recipes for Those Who Want
More with Just a Little Less

Jessica Seinfeld
and SARA QUESSENBERRY

New York London Toronto Sydney New Delhi

Gallery Books

An Imprint of Simon & Schuster, LLC
1230 Avenue of the Americas
New York, NY 10020

First Gallery Books hardcover edition November 2024

GALLERY BOOKS and colophon are registered trademarks of Simon & Schuster, LLC

Simon & Schuster: Celebrating 100 Years of Publishing in 2024

For information about special discounts for bulk purchases, please contact Simon & Schuster Special Sales at 1-866-506-1949 or business@simonandschuster.com.

The Simon & Schuster Speakers Bureau can bring authors to your live event. For more information or to book an event, contact the Simon & Schuster Speakers Bureau at 1-866-248-3049 or visit our website at www.simonspeakers.com.

Interior design by Laura Palese

Manufactured in China

10 9 8 7 6 5 4 3 2 1

Library of Congress Control Number: 2024016875

ISBN 978-1-6680-1536-0
ISBN 978-1-6680-1537-7 (ebook)

This book is dedicated to every kind of dessert lover. You won't know what you're missing.

Contents

Cookies & Bars

Cakes

Pies & Pastries

Fruit

Puddings, Custards & Ice Cream

A Quick Fix

Essential Recipes

Introduction

I've spent my whole life "saving room" for dessert, eagerly anticipating a sweet finish to a savory meal.

I love the excitement that dessert brings to daily life. A weeknight dinner feels a little more special topped off by dessert. These simple pleasures are important—they are the small rewards we look forward to every day.

Dessert is how we recognize those important, big days, too. Dessert goes hand in hand with the celebrations, special occasions, and social gatherings that matter most to us. These are the events in life where we create lasting memories and deepen social connections. Wedding and birthday cakes are the requisite finale to traditional life cycle moments. They are the final bow at the end, acknowledging something big has happened to someone you care about. We need these moments in our lives.

Many desserts are deeply rooted in cultural traditions and family recipes. Making and eating them evoke feelings of nostalgia and a connection to our childhoods and heritage. That's where it started for me: by the age of eight, I could turn out a perfect Duncan Hines devil's food cake. I've grown up to become someone who loves to make desserts from scratch, but if it weren't for the role Duncan Hines played in my childhood, I wouldn't be writing this book. It was the gateway to a love of baking.

Desserts are also what some turn to in times of stress or sadness. They comfort us and make us smile on hard days. Dare I say, an indulgence can even temporarily lift the mood. What I love about the recipes in this book is that I can experience comfort without such a big sugar crash afterward.

That is not to say everyone is a dessert person. If you are not, I doubt you will have read this far. This book is written for those who want to continue the dessert tradition but do it more mindfully. If you are still reading, might you have a little voice telling you it is finally time to cut out some sugar? Join us.

Many of us are somewhat educated on excess sugar's impact on our bodies. Overconsumption of processed, added sugars has been linked to various health issues, including obesity, type 2 diabetes, heart disease, and, as our parents always warned us, dental problems. I don't know about you, but I generally feel better when I eat less sugar. I have more energy, feel emotionally balanced, and don't crave unhealthy, sugary, or salty foods. As I've gotten older, I eat sweets less often than I used to. When I want the dessert experience, I now opt for something that doesn't leave me with that sticky-sweet hangover feeling. This book's recipes are just that: full of flavor and fun but made with less sugar. You won't have thoughts of regret.

In my first book, *Deceptively Delicious*, I added fruit and vegetables to boost sweetness, fiber, and nutritional density. I used fruit purees in place of processed sugar to sweeten desserts. That premise is the basis for *Not Too Sweet*. This book offers recipes with lots of naturally occurring sugars, especially fresh, dried, and frozen fruits; vegetables; maple syrup; honey; and date syrup. You'll find processed sugar in some recipes, but significantly less than in typical versions.

We have tested these recipes dozens of times to eliminate and decrease sugar and to lessen the number of steps needed to complete the recipe. The results are desserts you will love. They are easy to make and very satisfying—but Not Too Sweet.

Pantry

Oils and Butters

- Extra virgin olive oil: The least refined of all the oils. Choose an everyday, mild type that isn't too expensive.

- Coconut oil: We like an unrefined virgin coconut oil with its pronounced coconut flavor for baking.

- Unsalted butter: Since salt quantity varies from brand to brand, always use unsalted butter for baking. We like Cabot Creamery.

- Vegan butter: We use Miyoko's Creamery.

- Nonstick vegetable oil cooking spray

Plant-Based Milks, Dairy, and Eggs

- Unsweetened plant-based milk, such as oat, almond, or cashew: We used store-bought milks to develop these recipes. We found the best results with Oatly when making Oat Milk Caramel (page 224).

- Unsweetened coconut milk (full fat): Make sure the entire can of coconut milk (the thick top layer of coconut cream and the coconut milk) is emulsified before measuring by either shaking the unopened can or pouring into a bowl and whisking.

- Unsweetened coconut cream: Mostly contains coconut cream with a little coconut milk. (The inverse is true of coconut milk.)

- Heavy whipping cream: Also labeled as heavy cream.

- Whole milk: Full-fat cow's milk.

- Block cream cheese: Not the whipped kind. We use Philadelphia.

- Yogurt: Unsweetened 2% or 5% Greek (we love Fage) and plain yogurt. Or plant-based yogurt, such as almond, oat, or cashew.

- Sour cream: Full fat.

- Large eggs: Room-temperature eggs mix into batters more evenly than cold eggs. Note that it's easier to separate eggs when they're cold, but the whites whip up better at room temperature.

Dry Goods

- Gluten-free baking flour: We used Bob's Red Mill 1 to 1 Baking Flour to develop these recipes. We love the flavor, consistency, ease, and availability.

- Super-fine almond flour: We use Bob's Red Mill.

- All-purpose flour: Use your favorite brand. We like Gold Medal and King Arthur.

- Gluten-free old-fashioned rolled oats: As you can see, we are big fans of Bob's Red Mill.

- Unsweetened shredded coconut

- Unsweetened coconut flakes

- Baking powder

- Baking soda

- Cornstarch

Chocolate

- Dark chocolate chips: Cacao percentage is a matter of taste. The higher the percentage of cacao, the lower the amount of sugar and the more intense the chocolate flavor. We use 60% to 63% cacao chocolate chips in the recipes. Note: Dark chocolate is dairy-free, but not always vegan.

- Dark chocolate bar: We use 70% cacao chocolate bars for chopping and shaving.

- Unsweetened cocoa powder: We use natural cocoa powder, not Dutch processed.

Sweeteners

- Pure maple syrup: The darker the syrup, the stronger the maple flavor. We like the amber grade of syrup—it's rich but not overpowering.

- Honey: Choose a mild honey, such as clover.

- Date syrup: Made only with dates, it tastes like a mild molasses.

- Date sugar: Dried, ground dates.

- Coconut sugar: Made from the sap of the coconut palm tree. It tastes like a robust brown sugar.

- Granulated sugar: White sugar made from refined sugarcane.

- Confectioners' sugar: Also known as powdered sugar. Sugarcane is finely ground into a powder and blended with either cornstarch or tapioca starch to keep it from caking.

Dried Fruit

- Medjool dates: Plump and tender with a maple flavor, Medjool dates are great for baking and snacking.

- White Turkish figs: Also known as Smyrna figs. We love them for their sweet, mellow flavor with notes of vanilla and bourbon and soft, chewy texture.

- Dried apricots: We use the bright orange dried apricots for their pretty appearance in our frostings and fillings.

- Prunes: The delicious plums used for prunes, not your usual plums from the grocery store, are grown specifically for drying.

- Golden raisins: We prefer the mild, fruity flavor of golden raisins over dark raisins.

- Dried cherries: Unsweetened.

- Freeze-dried strawberries: Crisp, not chewy. No additives.

Extracts

- Pure vanilla extract: Unfortunately, you get what you pay for, but it's worth it. We like Nielsen-Massey and Rodelle.

- Pure almond extract: A little goes a long way.

Spices

- Ground cinnamon

- Ground cloves

- Cinnamon sticks: Great for flavoring slow-cooked desserts, like rice pudding and stewed fruits.

- Whole nutmeg: Whole nutmeg has a much fresher flavor than pre-ground nutmeg. Use a fine grater, such as a Microplane, to grate.

- Anise seeds: Sweet licorice flavor.

- Star anise: Not the same as anise seeds, but it has a similar licorice flavor, only stronger. A little goes a long way. Great for flavoring slow-cooked desserts.

- Kosher salt: We prefer Diamond Crystal.

Produce

- Citrus
- Fresh and frozen fruit
- Fresh ginger
- Fresh rosemary
- Sweet potato

Nuts and Seeds

Store nuts and seeds in an airtight container in the freezer or refrigerator to preserve freshness.

- Almonds: Raw or roasted
- Cashews: Raw
- Pecans: Raw
- Pine nuts: Raw
- Walnuts: Raw
- Hazelnuts: You can buy already roasted hazelnuts. Or roast them yourself for 15 minutes in a 350°F oven. Remove the skins by rubbing the hazelnuts together in a dry dish towel.
- Chia seeds and chia powder: A great source of omega-3 and dietary fiber. We use chia to thicken our chocolate pudding and the filling in our raspberry patties.
- Flaxseeds: Whole.
- Flaxseed meal: Made of finely ground flaxseeds. Mixed with water, it's a great vegan substitute for eggs in some baking recipes.
- Sesame seeds: Raw

Canned and Jarred

- Peanut butter: Creamy, unsweetened if you can find it, no-stir.

- Almond butter: Unsweetened, no-stir, and lightly toasted.

- Unsweetened applesauce: The ingredient list should contain apples only.

- Pumpkin puree: The ingredient list should contain pumpkin only.

- Chickpeas: Choose low-sodium or no salt. And save the aquafaba (the liquid in the can of chickpeas) to make vegan meringues.

- Fruit spreads: Fruit spreads have the least amount of sugar of the jam family. We like the St. Dalfour brand.

Equipment

Baking Equipment

- Stand mixer or hand mixer

- Two 8-inch (20-cm) round anodized aluminum (nonreactive and light color) cake pans: Thicker pans allow cakes to rise more evenly than thinner cake pans do and won't cause the cake to dome. We like Fat Daddio's. Hand wash.

- 9-inch (23-cm) round anodized aluminum cake pan

- 9 × 3-inch (23 × 7.5-cm) nonstick springform cake pan

- 8-inch (20-cm) square anodized aluminum baking pan

- 8½ x 4½-inch (22 × 11-cm) anodized aluminum loaf pan

- 10-inch (25-cm) tart pan with a removable bottom

- 10-cup nonstick Bundt pan

- Standard 12-cup cupcake pan

- Ceramic soufflé dish (about 8 × 3½ inches; 20 × 9 cm)

- Medium size (8 × 11-inch; 20 × 28-cm) nonreactive baking dish (glass or ceramic)

- Mixing bowls: A nesting set of three will do the trick (2.5-quart, 1.5-quart, and 1-quart; 2.5-liter, 1.5-liter, and 1-liter)

- Dry measuring cups

- Liquid measuring cups (2-cup and 4-cup; 500-ml and 1-liter)

- Measuring spoons

- Small offset metal spatula: For frosting cakes.

- Rolling pin: Choose any style that's comfortable. Wipe clean with a damp towel; don't submerge in water.

- Two wire cooling racks

- Set of round straight-edge cookie cutters

- Digital kitchen scale: One that weighs ounces and grams.

Multipurpose Equipment

- Food processor (11-cup or 14-cup)

- Blender: Regular or handheld.

- Whisk: An 11-inch balloon whisk is a good utility size.

- Silicone spatula: Silicone is great for its heat resistance.

- Metal spatula: For lifting cookies from sheet pans.

- Wooden spoon: Hand wash.

- 6- or 8-inch (15- or 20-cm) chef's knife: Hand wash all knives.

- Paring knife and serrated knife

- Fine grater: We like a Microplane.

- Stainless-steel strainer

- Citrus juicer

- Vegetable peeler

- Cutting board

- Two large rimmed aluminum (half) sheet pans (18 × 13-inch; 46 × 33-cm): We like Nordic Ware. Hand wash.

- One small rimmed aluminum (quarter) sheet pan (13 × 9-inch; 33 × 23-cm)

- 10-inch (25-cm) cast-iron skillet: Hand wash.

- 8-inch (20-cm) nonstick skillet

- Parchment paper: Precut sheets make life so much easier.

- Ruler or measuring tape

A Few Baking Tips

SETTING UP: Give yourself plenty of space. Clear your counter and set up your station with the equipment and ingredients you'll need for the recipe. Read the entire recipe the whole way through before getting started.

BE METHODICAL: Set up your ingredients on your left side. Once you've used them, set them to the right (or vice versa, if that's more comfortable). This way you won't lose track of what you've added and what you haven't.

MEASURING: For dry ingredients like flour and cocoa powder, first fluff with a spoon so it's not compact, then spoon a heaping amount into the measuring cup and swipe off the extra with a straight edge (like a knife) to level. It's important to keep the flour light and fluffy. Don't shake or pack in the flour to level it. If measuring smaller amounts, dip the measuring spoon into, for example, the baking powder, then level the top. Take your time. (Alternatively, for the most precise measurements, weigh the ingredients with a digital kitchen scale instead of using measuring cups.)

USE THE RIGHT EQUIPMENT: Use a silicone spatula, not a spoon, for scraping cake batter into cake pans so you get every last drop out of the bowl. It's also the perfect tool for folding in egg whites and mixing batters. The large blade and straight edge ensure that no part goes unmixed. Use a liquid measuring cup for liquids. Use dry measuring cups for dry ingredients. It sounds obvious, but it's important. Above all, know that the right equipment doesn't have to be the most expensive.

PREHEAT THE OVEN: To make sure your oven is properly heated, let the oven stand at the desired temperature for at least 15 minutes before using.

USE AN OVEN THERMOMETER: It's important to know that your oven is working at the right temperature. An inexpensive oven thermometer will show you that your oven is properly calibrated. But even still, oven temperatures fluctuate, and the way they heat can vary from brand to brand and, certainly, between gas and electric. That's why it's important to always check for visual cues in baking, not just follow baking times. You probably know if your oven runs hot or cool, so when you see a range for baking times, you can figure out where you fall.

GLUTEN-FREE BAKING: Most of the recipes in this book are gluten-free, using Bob's Red Mill 1 to 1 Baking Flour or super-fine almond flour. If you're new to this world, the biggest difference is with mixing. You can be overly zealous when mixing our cake batters, cookie doughs, and pie crusts and still get a tender result. This is contrary to working with all-purpose flour, where overmixing is to be avoided because overworking glutens (which give structure and strength) leads to tough or rubbery results. Another big difference has to do with our gluten-free cakes and testing for doneness. Because most gluten-free flours don't absorb moisture as well as all-purpose flour does, you are less likely to overbake a cake. So, if you're still in doubt that the cake is done, you can err on the side of adding a couple of extra minutes without the risk of a dry cake.

SUBSTITUTIONS: It's always tempting to substitute ingredients, change up the recipe, or add a little more of this and that. Most of the time, when cooking savory recipes you can get away with it. But resist this urge when baking, especially when it comes to chemistry. Switching from cinnamon to nutmeg is okay, but using baking soda instead of baking powder will ruin Grandma's birthday.

Cookies & Bars

Peanut Crunch Cookies

As a Girl Scout, I did a swift business selling Samoas. Crunchy, slightly chewy, these cookies remind me of them.

MAKES 16

1 cup (146 g) salted peanuts, coarsely chopped

1 cup (60 g) unsweetened coconut flakes

2/3 cup (115 g) dark chocolate chips

6 tablespoons (90 ml) Oat Milk Caramel (page 224)

1. Position an oven rack in the middle of the oven. Preheat the oven to 350°F. Line a large rimmed sheet pan with parchment paper.

2. In a medium bowl, stir together the peanuts, coconut flakes, chocolate chips, and Oat Milk Caramel until everything is well coated and evenly distributed.

3. For each cookie, spoon a 2-tablespoon mound of the mixture onto the prepared pan, spacing them about 1 inch apart. (Don't worry—once baked, the cookies will hold together.)

4. Bake for 12 to 14 minutes, until the cookies are set and golden brown around the edges. Place the pan on a wire cooling rack and let the cookies cool completely in the pan. Keep stored in an airtight container for up to 4 days.

Plum Caramel Shortbread Sandwich Cookies

For the filling, use bright-red dried plums, if you can find them, for their pretty color; otherwise, prunes are just as delicious. Or the shortbread on its own is the perfect wafer cookie for any occasion.

MAKES 14

Shortbread

1 recipe Gluten-Free Shortbread Dough with anise seeds (page 228)

Gluten-free baking flour, for rolling

Plum Caramel Filling

½ cup (80 g) dried pitted plums/prunes (about 10)

About 2 cups (480 ml) boiling water, for plumping the plums

2 tablespoons heavy whipping cream

1½ tablespoons pure maple syrup

⅛ teaspoon kosher salt

1. Position an oven rack in the middle of the oven. Preheat the oven to 350°F. Line a large rimmed sheet pan with parchment paper.

2. For the shortbread: Let the cold dough rest at room temperature for about 15 minutes, or until pliable for easy rolling. Lightly flour a large piece of parchment paper. Using a rolling pin, roll out the dough to a scant ¼ inch thick, adding more flour as necessary, to prevent sticking on top and underneath.

3. Using a round cookie cutter about 1¾ inches wide, cut out rounds from the dough and place on the prepared pan, spacing them 1 inch apart. Reroll the scraps, cut, and place them on the pan as well. Refrigerate for 10 minutes.

4. Bake the cookies for 14 to 18 minutes, until the undersides are light golden brown. Place the pan on a wire cooling rack. Let the cookies cool in the pan for 5 minutes, then transfer them to the wire rack and let cool completely.

5. For the plum caramel filling: Put the dried plums in a small mixing bowl. Add the boiling water to cover them by 1 inch and let stand for 10 minutes, or until softened. Drain and shake out excess water. Let cool completely.

6. In a food processor or blender, combine the plums, cream, maple syrup, and salt. Puree for 1 to 2 minutes, scraping down the sides as necessary with a silicone spatula, until creamy and thick like peanut butter.

7. To form the cookies, sandwich 2 cookies with about 1 teaspoon of the plum caramel filling. Keep stored in an airtight container for up to 1 week.

Date Graham Crackers

They stand beautifully on their own. But for a bigger experience
I'd pair them with roasted berries and cream cheese.

MAKES 18

½ cup (60 g) all-purpose flour, spooned and leveled

½ cup (66 g) whole-wheat flour, spooned and leveled

¾ teaspoon ground cinnamon

¼ teaspoon finely grated nutmeg

½ teaspoon kosher salt

¼ teaspoon baking powder

¼ teaspoon baking soda

3 tablespoons cold unsalted butter or vegan butter, cut into small pieces

3 tablespoons date syrup

2 tablespoons coconut milk, well shaken or whisked

1 teaspoon pure vanilla extract

Roasted Strawberries (page 225) or Roasted Blueberries (page 234), for serving

Cream cheese (vegan, if desired), for serving

1. In a food processor, pulse together the all-purpose flour, whole-wheat flour, cinnamon, nutmeg, salt, baking powder, and baking soda. Add the butter and pulse several times until the mixture resembles coarse cornmeal.

2. In a small bowl, whisk together the date syrup, coconut milk, and vanilla. Add to the food processor. Pulse several times until the mixture comes together into a big ball.

3. Transfer the dough to a large piece of plastic wrap, then shape it into a ½-inch-thick rectangle. Wrap tightly and refrigerate for at least 30 minutes.

4. Position an oven rack in the middle of the oven. Preheat the oven to 325°F. Line a large rimmed sheet pan with parchment paper.

5. Let the cold dough rest at room temperature for about 15 minutes, or until pliable for easy rolling.

6. Using a rolling pin, roll out the dough between 2 large pieces of parchment paper as evenly as you can to a scant ¼ inch thick. Cut the dough into about 1¾ x 2¼-inch rectangles and place them on the prepared pan, spacing them 1 inch apart. Gather up the scraps and repeat. (Alternatively, make it really easy and use a cookie cutter—any shape.)

7. Refrigerate for 10 minutes. Prick the tops several times with the tines of a fork.

8. Bake for 20 to 25 minutes, depending on thickness, until crisp and beginning to brown around the edges. Using a metal spatula, lift the cookies onto a wire cooling rack and let cool completely. They will crisp up more as they cool.

9. Serve with Roasted Strawberries or Roasted Blueberries (or both) and cream cheese. Keep stored in an airtight container for up to 2 weeks.

Apricot Rugelach

Without question, these are worth your time and energy to make.
I like to make them bite-size, for a perfect brunch treat.

MAKES 32

Dough

1 cup (148 g) gluten-free baking flour, spooned and leveled, plus more for rolling

1/4 teaspoon kosher salt

1 stick (8 tablespoons; 4 ounces; 113 g) cold unsalted butter, cut into small pieces

4 ounces (113 g) cold block cream cheese, cut into small pieces

1/2 teaspoon pure vanilla extract

Filling

1/2 cup (64 g) walnuts

2/3 cup (175 g) Apricot Puree (page 229)

6 teaspoons coconut sugar

1/2 teaspoon ground cinnamon

1 large egg, beaten

1. For the dough: In a food processor, combine the flour, salt, butter, cream cheese, and vanilla. Let the processor run for about 30 seconds, or until large moist crumbs form. Pour the crumbs onto a large piece of plastic wrap and knead a few times to bring the dough together. Divide in half. Shape into two balls, then press into 1/2-inch-thick smooth disks. Wrap each tightly with plastic wrap. Refrigerate for at least 30 minutes and up to 2 days.

2. Let the cold dough rest at room temperature for about 15 minutes, or until pliable for easy rolling.

3. Position an oven rack in the middle of the oven. Preheat the oven to 350°F. Line a large rimmed sheet pan with parchment paper.

4. For the filling: Spread the walnuts on a small rimmed sheet pan and bake for 6 to 8 minutes, until fragrant and crisp. Let cool, then finely chop. Put 2 tablespoons of the walnuts in a small bowl and the remaining larger quantity of walnuts in another bowl. Set aside.

5. Lightly flour a large piece of parchment paper. Using a rolling pin, roll out one disk of dough into a 10-inch circle (about 1/8 inch thick), adding a little more flour, as necessary, to prevent sticking on top and underneath.

6. Spoon on 1/3 cup (87 g) of the Apricot Puree and, with the back of the spoon, spread a thin layer over the dough, leaving a 1/2-inch border around the edges. Sprinkle half of the large amount of walnuts over the puree. Then sprinkle with 2 teaspoons of the coconut sugar and 1/4 teaspoon of the cinnamon.

7. Using a chef's knife or a pizza cutter, cut the circle into 4 triangles. Then cut each triangle into 4 smaller triangles. Starting from the outside edge, roll up each triangle as tightly as you can. Place on the prepared pan, spacing them 1 inch apart, with the little points facing down. Refrigerate. Repeat this process with the remaining dough and filling, then refrigerate for 10 minutes.

8. Lightly brush the tops of the rugelach with the beaten egg. Sprinkle with the remaining 2 tablespoons walnuts and 2 teaspoons coconut sugar.

9. Bake the rugelach for 25 to 30 minutes, until light golden brown. Place the pan on a wire cooling rack and let the cookies cool completely on the pan. Keep stored in an airtight container for up to 1 week.

Peanut Butter and Chocolate Bars

We let the date syrup do the sweetening here.

MAKES 16

Nonstick vegetable oil cooking spray

Crust

1 recipe Gluten-Free Shortbread Dough
(page 228)

Filling

½ cup (128 g) smooth peanut butter

¼ cup (60 ml) date syrup

⅛ teaspoon kosher salt

Topping

⅔ cup (115 g) dark chocolate chips
(vegan, if desired)

2 teaspoons coconut oil

1. Position an oven rack in the middle of the oven. Preheat the oven to 350°F. Spray an 8-inch square metal baking pan with cooking spray. Line the bottom and up all four sides with parchment paper, leaving 1-inch overhangs.

2. For the crust: Firmly press the Shortbread Dough evenly over the bottom of the prepared pan. Refrigerate for 30 minutes.

3. Bake the crust for 22 to 25 minutes, until set and light golden brown. Place the pan on a wire cooling rack and let cool for 10 minutes.

4. For the filling: In a small bowl, stir together the peanut butter, date syrup, and salt. Spread evenly over the warm crust, then let cool completely.

5. For the topping: In a small microwave-safe glass bowl, combine the chocolate chips and coconut oil. Melt in 10-second intervals, stirring each time, until melted and smooth, being careful not to overheat the chocolate. Or melt in a heat-proof glass bowl set over a pan of simmering water (don't let the bowl touch the water). Spread evenly over the filling. Refrigerate for about 15 minutes, or until the chocolate is set.

6. Grab the edges of the parchment and lift the square onto a cutting board. Slice into squares or bars. Keep stored in an airtight container in a cool place or in the refrigerator for up to 1 week.

Lemon Pistachio Cookies

This recipe is based on one of my favorites, called the Caprilu cookie, found in southern Italy. They are easy to make and even easier to eat. Compared to the traditional version, these have a fraction of the sugar.

MAKES 16

¾ cup (90 g) raw, shelled pistachios

¼ cup (46 g) coconut sugar

1¼ cups (135 g) super-fine almond flour, spooned and leveled

¼ teaspoon kosher salt

Finely grated zest of 1 lemon

1 large egg white

1 tablespoon fresh lemon juice

2 tablespoons honey

½ teaspoon pure vanilla extract

½ teaspoon pure almond extract

¼ cup (29 g) confectioners' sugar, spooned and leveled, plus more for rolling

1. In a food processor, combine the pistachios and coconut sugar. Pulse several times until finely chopped. Pour into a medium mixing bowl. Add the almond flour, salt, and lemon zest and stir together, making sure no lumps of almond flour remain.

2. In a small mixing bowl, using a fork, beat the egg white just to break it up. Stir in the lemon juice, honey, vanilla, and almond extract. Pour into the pistachio mixture and stir well until evenly incorporated (it will be a little sticky). Refrigerate the dough for 30 minutes.

3. Position an oven rack in the middle of the oven. Preheat the oven to 350°F. Line a large rimmed sheet pan with parchment paper.

4. Dust your work surface with a little confectioners' sugar. Gather up the chilled dough and shape it into a ball. Roll it in the confectioners' sugar, then shape it into a 16-inch-long log. Cut the log crosswise into 1-inch-wide pieces. Roll each piece between the palms of your hands to shape into a ball.

5. Put the ¼ cup of confectioners' sugar in a shallow bowl. Roll the balls in the confectioners' sugar to lightly coat. With your thumb and forefinger, give them a little squeeze in the middle to make them oblong with little indentations.

6. Place the cookies on the prepared sheet pan, spacing them 1 inch apart (they won't spread). Bake for 14 to 18 minutes, until set and light golden brown underneath and at the edges. Place the pan on a wire cooling rack and let the cookies cool completely in the pan. Keep stored in an airtight container for up to 1 week.

Almond-Ginger Shortbread

This one's for you, ginger lovers. Combined with not-too-sweet caramel and toasted almonds, it's heaven on Earth.

MAKES 16

Nonstick vegetable oil cooking spray

Crust

1 recipe Gluten-Free Shortbread Dough (page 228)

Filling

3/4 cup (66 g) sliced almonds

1 recipe Oat Milk Caramel (page 224)

2 tablespoons finely grated peeled fresh ginger

1. Position an oven rack in the middle of the oven. Preheat the oven to 350°F. Spray a 9-inch springform pan or a 9-inch tart pan with a removable bottom with cooking spray.

2. For the crust: Firmly press the Shortbread Dough evenly over the bottom and 1/4 inch up the sides of the prepared pan. Refrigerate for 30 minutes.

3. Bake the crust for 18 to 22 minutes, until set and light golden brown. Place the pan on a wire cooling rack and let cool.

4. For the filling: On a small rimmed sheet pan, spread out the almonds. Bake for 8 to 10 minutes, until light golden brown.

5. In a small saucepan, combine the Oat Milk Caramel, ginger, and almonds and stir to combine. Place over medium heat to warm it up. Scrape the mixture over the prepared crust and spread evenly. Bake for 15 to 20 minutes, until the caramel just starts to bubble.

6. Place the pan on a wire cooling rack and let cool completely. Remove the ring of the pan and slide the shortbread onto a cutting board. Slice into thin wedges. Keep stored in an airtight container for up to 1 week.

Lacy Flax Cookies

Hear me out: they may look healthy, but they taste anything but.
Maple syrup and cinnamon make an inviting combination in this easy
recipe. Traditional lace cookies have loads of sugar. Not these guys.

MAKES 18

¼ cup (41 g) golden flaxseeds

¼ cup (41 g) dark flaxseeds

½ cup (120 ml) cold water

2 tablespoons pure maple syrup

1 teaspoon ground cinnamon

Small pinch of kosher salt

2 tablespoons hemp seeds

1 cup (170 g) dark chocolate chips (vegan, if desired)

1 teaspoon coconut oil

1. Position two oven racks toward the middle of the oven. Preheat the oven to 250°F. Line two large rimmed sheet pans with parchment paper.

2. In a medium mixing bowl, stir together the golden and dark flaxseeds, water, maple syrup, cinnamon, and salt. Let stand, stirring occasionally, for 15 to 20 minutes, until the mixture is thick and gelatinous. Stir in the hemp seeds.

3. For each cookie, spoon a scant 1 tablespoon of the mixture onto the prepared pan. Using the back of a spoon, spread as evenly as you can into about a 2½-inch-wide circle. Repeat, spacing them about 1 inch apart.

4. Bake for about 1 hour, or until the cookies are dried out (they will crisp up as they cool). Place the pans on a wire cooling rack and let the cookies cool completely in the pans. Then peel the cookies from the parchment.

5. In a small microwave-safe glass bowl, combine the chocolate chips and coconut oil. Melt in 10-second intervals, stirring each time, until melted and smooth, being careful not to overheat the chocolate. Or melt in a heat-proof glass bowl set over a pan of simmering water (don't let the bowl touch the water).

6. Dip about one third of each cookie into the melted chocolate and shake off the excess. Place them back on the pans. Refrigerate for about 10 minutes, or until the chocolate is set. Keep stored in an airtight container in a cool place or in the refrigerator for up to 1 week.

Chocolate Chip Cookies

It's not a dessert book without a recipe for chocolate chip cookies. Even with all the "healthy" ingredients, these are wildly popular in my house.

MAKES 22

1 tablespoon flaxseed meal

2½ tablespoons cold water

2½ cups (270 g) super-fine almond flour, spooned and leveled

¾ teaspoon baking soda

¾ teaspoon kosher salt

1 stick (8 tablespoons; 4 ounces; 113g) unsalted butter or vegan butter, at cool room temperature

½ cup (92 g) coconut sugar

¼ cup (60 ml) pure maple syrup

1½ teaspoons pure vanilla extract

1½ cups (256 g) dark chocolate chips (vegan, if desired)

1. Position two oven racks toward the middle of the oven. Preheat the oven to 350°F. Line two large rimmed sheet pans with parchment paper.

2. In a small bowl, combine the flaxseed meal and water. Let stand for about 10 minutes, or until thickened.

3. In a medium mixing bowl, whisk together the almond flour, baking soda, and salt, making sure no lumps of almond flour remain.

4. In the bowl of a stand mixer fitted with the paddle attachment, or in a large mixing bowl with a hand mixer, beat together the butter and coconut sugar until fluffy, about 2 minutes. Add the maple syrup, vanilla, and the flaxseed mixture and beat until creamy and well combined, scraping down the sides as necessary with a silicone spatula. Add the dry ingredients and mix in on medium-low speed.

5. Stir in the chocolate chips.

6. Scoop 2-tablespoon mounds of dough onto the prepared pans, spacing them 2 inches apart. Bake for 15 to 18 minutes, until light golden brown and just set in the middle. Place the pans on wire cooling racks and let the cookies cool for 10 minutes. Using a metal spatula, transfer the cookies to the cooling rack. Serve warm or let cool completely. Keep stored in an airtight container for up to 4 days.

Peanut Butter and Jelly Thumbprint Cookies

One bowl, quick prep, and a winning flavor combo—
you will make these all the time. These cover a lot of ground:
they are vegan, gluten-free, and low-sugar.

MAKES 22

¼ cup (60 ml) pure maple syrup

¼ cup (64 g) smooth peanut butter, plus more for filling the thumbprints

2 tablespoons coconut oil, melted

1 teaspoon pure vanilla extract

½ teaspoon kosher salt

¼ teaspoon baking powder

¼ teaspoon baking soda

2 cups (216 g) super-fine almond flour, spooned and leveled

Strawberry fruit spread, for filling the thumbprints

1. Position an oven rack in the middle of the oven. Preheat the oven to 350°F. Line a large rimmed sheet pan with parchment paper.

2. In a medium mixing bowl, whisk together the maple syrup, peanut butter, coconut oil, and vanilla. Then whisk in the salt, baking powder, and baking soda. Add the almond flour and, using a wooden spoon, stir until well combined and no almond flour lumps remain.

3. For each cookie, scoop out 1 tablespoon of dough and, using the palms of your hands, roll it into a ball. Space them about 2 inches apart on the prepared pan. Use your thumb to make a deep indentation (thumbprint) in the middle of each ball.

4. Spoon a tiny amount of peanut butter (about ⅛ teaspoon) into the thumbprints. Then fill with the strawberry fruit spread.

5. Bake for 12 to 14 minutes, until light golden brown and set around the edges. Place the pan on a wire cooling rack and let the cookies cool for 10 minutes. Using a metal spatula, lift the cookies onto the rack and let cool completely. Keep stored in an airtight container for up to 4 days.

Lemon Bars

Typical lemon bars have at least a cup of sugar. We use maple syrup,
and they still maintain a rich, lemony flavor and texture.

MAKES 16

Nonstick vegetable oil cooking spray

Crust

1 recipe Gluten-Free Shortbread Dough
(page 228)

Filling

2 to 3 lemons

1 navel orange

2 large eggs

3 large egg yolks

1 tablespoon cornstarch

½ cup (120 ml) pure maple syrup

¼ teaspoon kosher salt

3 tablespoons cold unsalted butter or
vegan butter

1. Position an oven rack in the middle of the oven. Preheat the oven to
350°F. Spray an 8-inch square metal baking pan with cooking spray. Line
the bottom and up all four sides with parchment paper, leaving 1-inch
overhangs.

2. For the crust: Firmly press the Shortbread Dough evenly over the
bottom of the prepared pan. Refrigerate for 30 minutes.

3. Bake the crust for 22 to 25 minutes, until set and light golden brown.
Place the pan on a wire cooling rack and let cool.

4. For the filling: Finely grate 1 teaspoon of zest from a lemon (or two) and
finely grate ½ teaspoon of zest from the orange; set aside. Squeeze the
lemons to yield ½ cup (120 ml) juice. Squeeze the orange to yield ¼ cup
(60 ml) juice.

5. In a small saucepan, whisk together the eggs and egg yolks, then whisk
in the cornstarch. Add the maple syrup, salt, lemon juice, and orange juice
and whisk together.

6. Place the saucepan over medium heat. Whisk often as the filling heats
up, making sure to get into the corners of the pan. Once it starts to bubble,
whisk constantly for 1 minute more, until thickened. Remove the pan from
the heat.

7. Place a fine-mesh strainer over a small mixing bowl. Pour the filling
through the strainer to remove any lumps. Stir in the butter, lemon zest, and
orange zest.

8. Pour the filling over the prepared crust and spread evenly. Bake for
10 to 12 minutes, until the filling is set. Place the pan on the wire cooling
rack and let cool to room temperature. Then refrigerate for about 1 hour,
or until completely chilled.

9. Grab the edges of the parchment and lift the square onto a cutting
board. Slice into bars or squares. Keep stored in an airtight container in the
refrigerator for up to 4 days.

Figs in a Blanket

The name is not even the best part; these taste like your favorite
Fig Newtons, but made with better ingredients.

MAKES 24

Dough

1 cup (148 g) gluten-free baking flour, spooned and leveled, plus more for rolling

1 teaspoon finely grated orange zest

1/4 teaspoon kosher salt

1 stick (8 tablespoons; 4 ounces; 113 g) cold unsalted butter, cut into small pieces

4 ounces (113 g) cold block cream cheese, cut into small pieces

1/2 teaspoon pure vanilla extract

Filling

10 dried white Turkish figs (230 g), stems removed

2 to 3 tablespoons fresh orange juice

1/2 teaspoon pure vanilla extract

1/2 teaspoon ground cinnamon

Small pinch of kosher salt

1 large egg, beaten

1. For the dough: In a food processor, pulse together the flour, orange zest, and salt. Add the butter, cream cheese, and vanilla. Let the processor run for about 30 seconds, or until large moist crumbs form. Pour the crumbs onto a large piece of plastic wrap and knead a few times to bring the dough together. Divide in half and shape into two 1/2-inch-thick rectangles. Wrap each tightly with plastic wrap. Refrigerate for at least 30 minutes and up to 2 days.

2. Meanwhile, make the filling: Put the figs in a food processor and finely chop them. Add 2 tablespoons of the orange juice, the vanilla, cinnamon, and salt. Pulse until the mixture becomes a paste (it will come together into a ball). If it's a little dry, add the remaining 1 tablespoon orange juice.

3. Let the cold dough rest at room temperature for about 15 minutes, or until pliable for easy rolling.

4. Preheat the oven to 350°F. Line a large rimmed sheet pan with parchment paper.

5. Lightly flour a large piece of parchment paper. Using a rolling pin, roll out one rectangle of dough to about a 12 × 5-inch rectangle (about 1/8 inch thick), adding a little more flour, as necessary, to prevent sticking on top and underneath.

6. Using half of the filling, shape it into a log lengthwise down the middle of the rolled-out dough (wet fingertips help). Roll one long side of dough over the filling, then continue to roll into a log with the seam side down. Gently flatten to about 3/4 inch thick. Transfer to the prepared sheet pan and refrigerate while you repeat the process with the remaining dough and filling. Refrigerate for 10 minutes.

7. Lightly brush the tops of the logs with the beaten egg. Cut the logs crosswise into 1-inch-wide bars and arrange them on the pan, spacing them 1 inch apart.

8. Bake for 25 to 30 minutes, until light golden brown. Place the pan on a wire cooling rack and let the bars cool completely. Keep stored in an airtight container for up to 1 week.

Cherry Almond Biscotti

These crunchy, just-sweet-enough treats stay fresh for at least three weeks in the cookie jar. Enjoy them any time of day or, like I do, with your morning coffee.

MAKES 34

1¼ cups (150 g) all-purpose flour, spooned and leveled

½ cup (66 g) whole-wheat flour, spooned and leveled

½ teaspoon ground cinnamon

¼ teaspoon finely grated nutmeg

⅛ teaspoon freshly ground black pepper

½ teaspoon kosher salt

½ teaspoon baking powder

2 large eggs

¼ cup (46 g) coconut sugar

2 tablespoons extra virgin olive oil

Finely grated zest from 1 navel orange

1 teaspoon pure vanilla extract

1 tablespoon water, plus a little more, if necessary

½ cup (71 g) whole raw almonds

½ cup (80 g) dried cherries, coarsely chopped

8 dried white Turkish figs (184 g), stems removed, coarsely chopped

1. Position an oven rack in the middle of the oven. Preheat the oven to 350°F. Line a large rimmed sheet pan with parchment paper.

2. In a large mixing bowl, whisk together the all-purpose flour, whole-wheat flour, cinnamon, nutmeg, pepper, salt, and baking powder.

3. In a small mixing bowl, whisk together the eggs, coconut sugar, olive oil, orange zest, vanilla, and water. Pour over the dry ingredients and stir together until well combined and large moist clumps form. The dough should hold together when pinched and be a little sticky. If it's a little dry, sprinkle in another 1 to 2 teaspoons water.

4. Add the almonds, cherries, and figs to the dough and knead together in the bowl until evenly distributed.

5. Turn the dough onto your work surface and divide it in half. Shape each half into a 10-inch-long log and place it on the prepared pan. Flatten the tops of the logs so that when they are sliced, they will have that "biscotti" shape. (Since these cookies have less sugar added, they won't spread during baking like a typical biscotti, so you have to shape them before baking.)

6. Bake for 20 to 23 minutes, until they are set and the undersides are light golden brown. Place the pan on a wire cooling rack and let the logs cool in the pan for 25 minutes.

7. Reduce the oven temperature to 300°F.

8. Move the logs to a cutting board. Using a gentle sawing motion with a serrated knife, slice the logs crosswise into scant ½-inch-thick slices. (They can be a little fragile at this stage.) Lay the slices flat on the prepared sheet pan, spacing them close together. Bake for 30 to 40 minutes, until crisp and dried out. They will crisp up a little more as they cool, too. Turn off the oven. Prop open the oven door and let the biscotti continue to dry out as the oven cools.

9. Let the biscotti cool completely before storing. Keep stored in an airtight container for up to 3 weeks.

Blondies

The almond butter, applesauce, and cinnamon combo is what does it for me. It's worth mentioning that they are gluten-free, vegan, and not too sweet. You will make a lot of people happy when you make these.

MAKES 16

Nonstick vegetable oil cooking spray

1 tablespoon flaxseed meal

2½ tablespoons water

½ cup (120 ml) unsweetened applesauce

⅓ cup (85 g) smooth almond butter

¼ cup (60 ml) pure maple syrup

¼ cup (55 g) coconut oil, melted

3 tablespoons coconut sugar

2 teaspoons pure vanilla extract

1 cup (148 g) gluten-free baking flour, spooned and leveled

1 teaspoon baking powder

½ teaspoon baking soda

½ teaspoon kosher salt

½ teaspoon ground cinnamon

⅓ cup (57 g) finely chopped block chocolate or chopped dark chocolate chips (vegan, if desired)

1. Position an oven rack in the middle of the oven. Preheat the oven to 350°F. Spray an 8-inch square metal baking pan with cooking spray. Line the bottom and up two opposite sides with parchment paper, leaving 1-inch overhangs.

2. In a small bowl, stir together the flaxseed meal and water. Let stand for about 10 minutes, or until thickened.

3. In a large mixing bowl, whisk together the applesauce and almond butter. Add the maple syrup, coconut oil, coconut sugar, vanilla, and the flaxseed mixture and whisk until well combined. Add the flour, baking powder, baking soda, salt, and cinnamon. Whisk vigorously until well combined.

4. Use a silicone spatula to fold in the chopped chocolate. Scrape the batter into the prepared pan and spread evenly over the bottom of the pan.

5. Bake for 30 to 35 minutes, until springy to the touch and a toothpick inserted in the middle comes out clean. Place the pan on a wire cooling rack and let cool completely. Grab the edges of the parchment and lift the blondies onto a cutting board. Slice into squares and serve. Keep stored, tightly wrapped, for up to 4 days.

Chocolate Brownies

Using my original *Deceptively Delicious* tactics, we add
sweet potato and dates to serve up rich, delicious, fudgy gluten- and
grain-free brownies—with the bonus of some vitamin A.

MAKES 16

Nonstick vegetable oil cooking spray

1 medium sweet potato, such as garnet yam

10 Medjool dates (220 g), pitted

About 3 cups boiling water, for plumping the dates

1 large egg

¼ cup (60 ml) extra virgin olive oil

2 teaspoons pure vanilla extract

½ cup (54 g) super-fine almond flour, spooned and leveled

¼ cup (21 g) unsweetened cocoa powder, plus more for dusting

½ teaspoon baking soda

½ teaspoon kosher salt

½ cup (86 g) dark chocolate chips, melted

1. Position an oven rack in the middle of the oven. Preheat the oven to 400°F. Spray an 8-inch square metal baking pan with cooking spray. Line the bottom and up two opposite sides with parchment paper, leaving 1-inch overhangs.

2. Prick the sweet potato a few times with the tines of a fork. Place on a small rimmed sheet pan and bake for 35 to 45 minutes, until very tender. When cool enough to handle, scoop out the flesh and measure ¾ cup; save any remaining sweet potato for another use.

3. Reduce the oven temperature to 350°F.

4. Put the dates in a small mixing bowl. Cover with the boiling water by 1 inch and let stand for about 10 minutes, or until very soft. Drain and shake out excess water.

5. In a food processor, puree the dates and sweet potato together until very smooth. Add the egg, olive oil, and vanilla and pulse several times to combine. Then add the almond flour, cocoa powder, baking soda, and salt and pulse in.

6. In a small microwave-safe bowl, melt the chocolate chips in 10-second intervals, stirring each time, until melted and smooth, being careful not to overheat the chocolate. Or melt in a heat-proof glass bowl set over a pan of simmering water (don't let the bowl touch the water).

7. Add the melted chocolate to the batter and pulse until well incorporated (be sure to scrape down the sides and into the corners).

8. Scrape the batter into the prepared pan and spread evenly over the bottom of the pan.

9. Bake for 30 to 35 minutes, until springy to the touch and a toothpick inserted in the middle comes out clean. Place the pan on a wire cooling rack and let cool completely. Grab the edges of the parchment and lift the brownies onto a cutting board.

10. Dust with cocoa powder. Slice into squares and serve. Keep stored, tightly wrapped, for up to 4 days.

Brown Butter Almond Wafers

The brown butter crunch makes these irresistible. I keep them on the counter for passersby to enjoy any time of day.

MAKES ABOUT 52

4 tablespoons (2 ounces; 57 g) unsalted butter

⅓ cup (28 g) sliced raw almonds, finely chopped

½ cup (92 g) coconut sugar

1 cup (148 g) gluten-free baking flour, spooned and leveled

¼ teaspoon baking soda

¼ teaspoon kosher salt

3 tablespoons cold water

1. In a small skillet, melt the butter over medium heat. Add the almonds and cook, stirring constantly with a wooden spoon for 2 to 4 minutes, until the butter and almonds turn golden brown and smell nutty. Immediately scrape the mixture into a medium mixing bowl to stop the cooking. Let cool for 5 minutes, then stir in the coconut sugar.

2. In a small mixing bowl, whisk together the flour, baking soda, and salt. Add half of the flour mixture to the almond mixture and stir until well combined, then stir in the remaining flour mixture. Stir in the water until it resembles wet sand. Knead a few times in the bowl to bring the dough together into a ball.

3. On a large piece of parchment paper, use your hands to shape the dough into a 9-inch flat-sided or round log (depending on whether you prefer an oblong or round cookie when sliced). Wrap up in the parchment, then wrap tightly in plastic wrap. Refrigerate for at least 1 hour and up to 2 days, or you can freeze for up to 1 month.

4. Position two oven racks toward the middle of the oven. Preheat the oven to 325°F. Line two large rimmed sheet pans with parchment paper.

5. With a sharp knife, thinly and evenly slice the log crosswise into about ⅛-inch-thick cookies. Place the cookies about 1 inch apart on the prepared pans. Bake for 17 to 22 minutes, until they are set and dry to the touch. Place the pans on wire cooling racks and let the cookies cool completely in the pans. They will crisp as they cool. Keep stored in an airtight container for up to 3 weeks.

Chocolate Meringue Kisses

Let's use some of that leftover aquafaba from our Chocolate Layer Cake (page 66) and turn it into a vegan kiss.

MAKES ABOUT 70

One 15-ounce can chickpeas

½ cup (100 g) granulated sugar

¼ teaspoon cream of tartar

½ teaspoon ground cinnamon

1 teaspoon pure vanilla extract

1¼ cups (213 g) dark chocolate chips (vegan, if desired)

1 teaspoon coconut oil

1. Position two oven racks toward the middle of the oven. Preheat the oven to 250°F. Line two large rimmed sheet pans with parchment paper.

2. Place a strainer over the bowl of a stand mixer fitted with the whisk attachment or a large mixing bowl with a hand mixer. Drain the chickpeas, letting the aquafaba collect in the bottom of the bowl. You should get ½ cup to 2/3 cup (120 ml to 160 ml). Save the chickpeas for another use (like our Chocolate Layer Cake).

3. Add the sugar and cream of tartar to the aquafaba. Beat on high speed for 5 to 8 minutes, until stiff, shiny, voluminous peaks form. Then beat in the cinnamon and vanilla until well incorporated.

4. Scoop the meringue mixture into a pastry bag with a ½-inch tip. Or make your own bag: Scrape the mixture into a zip-top plastic bag and use scissors to cut a ½-inch hole in one of the corners.

5. Hold the bag vertically over the prepared pan without letting it touch the pan. Gently squeeze to make a small round about 1½ inches wide, then quickly pull away to form a peak. Repeat, spacing them about 1 inch apart.

6. Bake the meringues for 1 hour without opening the oven door, then rotate the pans 180° and switch from top to bottom. Bake for 15 to 30 minutes more, until the meringues are set, dry to the touch, and without any browning. (They will crisp up more as they cool.) Turn off the oven, prop the door open, and let the meringues continue to dry out as the oven cools. Place the pans on wire cooling racks and let the meringues cool completely in the pans.

7. In a small microwave-safe glass bowl, combine the chocolate chips and coconut oil. Melt in 10-second intervals, stirring each time, until melted and smooth, being careful not to overheat the chocolate. Or melt in a heat-proof glass bowl set over a pan of simmering water (don't let the bowl touch the water).

8. Dip the bottom of each kiss in the melted chocolate and, using the edge of the bowl, scrape off the excess chocolate. Place them back on the pans. (Reheat the chocolate as necessary.)

9. Refrigerate for about 10 minutes, or until the chocolate is set. Keep stored in an airtight container in a cool dry place or in the refrigerator for up to 2 weeks.

CHOCOLATE MERINGUE KISSES   56

A LECTURE ON SWEETNESS

You may be thinking, *How on earth can a chocolate cake with only half the sugar taste as good as one with the full amount of sugar?* I have news for the skeptics: it is easy for your taste buds to adjust to less sugar (the rest of your body will thank you, too).

Over the past few decades, consumer product companies have increased the sugar content in their foods. They use not only cane sugar but also various types of manufactured sugars to improve their products' taste, texture, and shelf life. Sucrose, high-fructose corn syrup, glucose, fructose, maltose, and lactose, as well as various sugar substitutes, are commonplace in processed foods on grocery store shelves. Various sugar substitutes and alternative sweeteners, such as stevia, erythritol, and aspartame, are used in products so that they can be marketed as "sugar-free" or "reduced sugar."

Humans love sweetness, so product manufacturers have capitalized on this and added sugar(s) to unlikely foods like bread, sauces, and condiments—not only the obvious ones, like baked goods, candies, and beverages. We now expect to have our socks knocked off at the end of a meal or when we have an afternoon treat because our taste buds and bloodstream are waiting for a sugar rush. So, it's our job to recognize this stealth trick of theirs and take back control of our sugar intake!

When you start paying attention to nutrition labels and how much sugar you are consuming, you might realize that you are on your way to a host of health issues, like diabetes, obesity, cardiovascular diseases, and dental problems. Some ways to turn this around are to assume everything you eat has more sugar than you think it does, cook more meals at home, and, of course, eat desserts from *Not Too Sweet*. Trust me, your taste buds and your body will adapt to and enjoy having less.

When I turned fifty, this happened naturally for me. I was lucky that I didn't have to work very hard to make drastic changes to cut down on sugar. I simply lost the desire for it. I continue to feel better and better as I eat less sugar. As people who have always finished their meals with dessert, creating recipes that were easy to make but made with less sugar was the next frontier for Sara and me.

If you want to join us not only as a dessert person but a responsible one, there is a whole new world of flavor open to you in *Not Too Sweet*. Sara and I have had fun experimenting with more healthful ways to sweeten so we don't rely on processed sugar. (Some of you may note similar tactics from my first book, *Deceptively Delicious*.)

In many of our recipes, to compensate for lower sugar amounts, we incorporate other flavors to add complexity and "trick" your palate into thinking something is sweet, such as:

- Warm spices like cinnamon, nutmeg, and star anise

- Citrus juice and zest

- Fresh ginger

- Fresh rosemary

- Unsweetened shredded and flaked coconut

We also use dried fruits, such as:

- Dried figs to sweeten our Figs in a Blanket (page 47)

- Apricot puree to sweeten Apricot Custard (page 184) and Whipped Apricot Frosting (page 78)

- Golden raisins to do all the sweetening in our Rosemary Shortcakes with Roasted Strawberries (page 225)

- Dried dates and date syrup to sweeten the Rice Pudding with Date Broiled Pineapple (page 180)

Nuts, like cashews and pecans, have their own natural sweetness, and we use:

- Cashew puree for the base in our Peanut Butter Ripple Ice Cream Pie (page 129)

- Pecans to sweeten the crust in the Sweet Potato Coconut Rum Tart (page 125)

Dairy- and plant-based milks have their own natural sweetness and richness. For example:

- We reduce oat milk with a little honey to make Oat Milk Caramel (page 224)

- Our Maple Whipped Cream (page 236) needs only a small amount of maple syrup to satisfy

- Whipped coconut cream needs no added sweetener in our Grilled Cardamom-Honey Plums with Coconut Cream (page 144)

- We use unsweetened Greek yogurt in our Frozen Yogurt with Cherry Compote and Chickpea Brittle (page 164)

Maple syrup, coconut sugar, and honey are the heroes of this book and are used to sweeten many of the recipes. While still sugars, they are more complex and less refined than granulated sugar. And we use much less of them here than traditional recipes do.

So, give it a chance. You will surprise yourself and your loved ones by proving that dessert can be delicious and luscious while not too sweet.

Cakes

Chocolate Layer Cake

Chickpeas and chocolate cake? You know I have a habit of
adding healthy, unexpected ingredients to our favorite foods to make
them more flavorful and nutrient-dense. The chickpeas make our
cake moist, but you can't taste them one bit.

SERVES 8 TO 10

Nonstick vegetable oil cooking spray

Cake

4 large eggs

Two 15-ounce cans chickpeas, drained
and rinsed (reserve the aquafaba for
Chocolate Meringue Kisses, page 56, or
Little Cherry Mousse Pies, page 130)

1 cup (240 ml) pure maple syrup

1/2 cup (120 ml) extra virgin olive oil

2 teaspoons pure vanilla extract

2 teaspoons instant espresso powder

1/4 cup (60 ml) hot water

3 cups (324 g) super-fine almond flour,
spooned and leveled

2/3 cup (56 g) unsweetened cocoa
powder

2 teaspoons baking soda

1 teaspoon kosher salt

Frosting

1 1/2 cups (240 g) pitted prunes (about 36)

About 3 cups boiling water, for plumping
the prunes

5 tablespoons pure maple syrup

1 1/2 cups (360 ml) heavy whipping cream

7 tablespoons (37 g) unsweetened cocoa
powder

1 1/2 teaspoons pure vanilla extract

1/4 teaspoon kosher salt

1. Position an oven rack in the middle of the oven. Preheat the oven to
350°F. Spray two 8-inch round metal cake pans with cooking spray. Line the
bottoms with parchment paper.

2. For the cake: In a large bowl, whisk together the eggs.

3. In a food processor, puree the chickpeas until very smooth, adding
up to 1/4 cup (60 ml) water, if necessary, to help smooth it out. Measure
2 cups (470 g) of the puree and whisk it into the eggs (save any extra
puree for another use). Add the maple syrup, olive oil, and vanilla and
whisk together.

4. In a small bowl, stir together the espresso powder with the hot water
until dissolved. (Alternatively, you can use 1/4 cup freshly brewed espresso.)
Whisk the espresso into the batter.

5. In a medium mixing bowl, whisk together the almond flour, cocoa
powder, baking soda, and salt until well combined and no almond flour
lumps remain. Add to the batter and whisk until well combined.

6. Dividing evenly, scrape the batter into the prepared pans. Bake for
34 to 40 minutes, until springy to the touch and a toothpick comes out
clean when inserted in the middle.

7. Place the pans on a wire cooling rack and let cool for 25 minutes. Run a
paring knife around the edges of the cakes to loosen them from the pans.
Invert the cakes onto the wire rack and remove the parchment paper. Flip
the cakes back over and let them cool completely.

8. For the frosting: Put the prunes in a small mixing bowl. Add the boiling
water to cover them by 1 inch. Let stand for 10 minutes, or until very soft.
Drain and shake out excess water. Let cool completely.

9. In a food processor, combine the prunes and maple syrup. Puree until
very smooth. Add the cream, cocoa powder, vanilla, and salt. Puree,
scraping down the sides as necessary, until smooth and creamy. If the
frosting feels at all warm or is a little too loose to frost, refrigerate for
10 to 15 minutes, until it sets up and becomes more spreadable.

10. To frost the cake, put one cake on a serving plate or cake stand. Frost the top with about 1 cup of the frosting. Place the other cake on top of it. Frost the top and sides of the cake. Slice and serve.

11. The frosted cake can be refrigerated for up to 2 days under a cake dome. Let the cake come to room temperature before serving. Any leftovers, tightly wrapped, will last even longer.

Lemon Bundt Cake

This is a special one. We use delicious coconut butter
(found easily online) in lieu of cups of confectioners' sugar to make
the icing rich and smooth. The tarty sweetness is a knockout.

SERVES 12 TO 15

Nonstick vegetable oil cooking spray

Cake

3 cups (444 g) gluten-free flour, spooned
and leveled

2 teaspoons baking powder

1 teaspoon baking soda

1½ teaspoons kosher salt

4 large eggs

1 cup (227 g) unsweetened Greek yogurt,
sour cream, or plant-based yogurt, such
as almond

1 cup (240 ml) extra virgin olive oil

¾ cup (180 ml) pure maple syrup

½ cup (92 g) coconut sugar

Finely grated zest of 2 lemons

¼ cup (60 ml) fresh lemon juice (from
1 to 2 lemons)

Icing

½ cup (120 g) coconut butter

¼ cup (60 ml) pure maple syrup

¼ cup (60 ml) coconut milk, well shaken
or whisked

Finely grated zest of 2 lemons, plus more
for topping (optional)

2 tablespoons fresh lemon juice

Small pinch of kosher salt

1. Position an oven rack in the middle of the oven. Preheat the oven to
350°F. Spray a 10-cup Bundt pan with cooking spray.

2. For the cake: In a medium mixing bowl, whisk together the flour, baking
powder, baking soda, and salt.

3. In a large mixing bowl, whisk together the eggs. Add the yogurt, olive
oil, maple syrup, and coconut sugar and whisk together. Next, whisk in the
lemon zest and lemon juice. Add the dry ingredients and whisk until well
combined.

4. Scrape the batter into the prepared pan and level the top. Bake for
53 to 58 minutes, until a toothpick inserted in the middle comes out with
a few moist crumbs. Place the pan on a wire cooling rack and let cool for
15 minutes, then unmold the cake. (It releases more easily while still quite
warm.) Let the cake cool completely on the wire rack.

5. For the icing: In a small saucepan, gently warm the coconut butter,
maple syrup, and coconut milk for about 30 seconds over low heat,
whisking constantly, until smooth and creamy (be careful not to overheat
because the coconut butter will melt completely). Remove from the heat
and whisk in the lemon zest, lemon juice, and salt. If it's a little too thick,
place over the heat to warm up a little more. If it's too thin to coat the cake,
let it cool down to the right thickness.

6. Immediately drizzle the icing over the top of the cake, letting it drip
down the sides. If desired, use a citrus zester to add lemon zest to the
top of the cake. Once the icing is set (about 15 minutes), slice and serve
the cake.

7. The cake will keep, tightly wrapped, at room temperature for up to
4 days.

Sweet Oat Cake

A cake you make in a blender—straightforward, less mess—
with lots of wholesome ingredients.

SERVES 8

Nonstick vegetable oil cooking spray

1½ cups (144 g) gluten-free old-fashioned rolled oats

4 large eggs

1 cup (220 g) cottage cheese

½ cup (40 g) unsweetened shredded coconut

⅓ cup (80 ml) pure maple syrup

⅓ cup (80 ml) extra virgin olive oil

1 teaspoon pure vanilla extract

2 teaspoons baking powder

½ teaspoon kosher salt

¾ cup (170 g) unsweetened plain yogurt, for serving

1 recipe Roasted Blueberries (page 234) or Roasted Strawberries (page 225), for serving

1. Position an oven rack in the middle of the oven. Preheat the oven to 350°F. Spray an 8½ x 4½-inch metal loaf pan with cooking spray. Line the bottom and up the two long sides with parchment paper, leaving 1-inch overhangs.

2. In a blender, blend the oats into a flour. Add the eggs, cottage cheese, shredded coconut, maple syrup, olive oil, vanilla, baking powder, and salt. Blend until well combined.

3. Scrape the batter into the prepared pan. Bake for 45 to 50 minutes, until a toothpick inserted in the middle comes out clean. Place the pan on a wire cooling rack and let cool for 25 minutes. Grab the edges of the parchment and lift the cake onto a cutting board and let cool completely.

4. Slice the cake, then divide among plates. Serve topped with the yogurt and Roasted Blueberries or Roasted Strawberries or a combination of both.

5. The cake will keep, tightly wrapped, at room temperature for up to 4 days.

Peach Cake

I love the peach, honey, and almond flavors in here. The apricot
that's spread on top is just the right finishing touch.

SERVES 8

Nonstick vegetable oil cooking spray

1¼ cups (185 g) gluten-free baking flour,
spooned and leveled

½ cup (54 g) super-fine almond flour,
spooned and leveled

3 tablespoons coconut sugar

2 teaspoons baking powder

½ teaspoon kosher salt

1 stick (8 tablespoons; 4 ounces; 113 g)
unsalted butter or vegan butter, at cool
room temperature

3 large eggs, beaten

5 tablespoons (75 ml) honey

½ teaspoon pure almond extract

2 ripe medium peaches or nectarines,
peeled, pitted, and quartered

2 tablespoons apricot fruit spread

1. Position an oven rack in the middle of the oven. Preheat the oven to
325°F. Spray a 9-inch springform pan with cooking spray.

2. In the bowl of a stand mixer fitted with the paddle attachment, or
in a large mixing bowl with a hand mixer, whisk together the baking
flour, almond flour, coconut sugar, baking powder, and salt until well
incorporated and no almond flour lumps remain. Add the butter. Beat
together on medium-low speed until the mixture resembles damp sand.

3. In a small mixing bowl, whisk together the eggs, 3 tablespoons of the
honey, and the almond extract. Add the mixture to the large bowl and beat
on medium-low speed for 30 seconds, until well combined, scraping down
the sides of the bowl with a silicone spatula as necessary.

4. Scrape the batter into the prepared pan and spread it evenly.

5. Slice each peach quarter crosswise into about ¼-inch-thick slices (hold
the ends together as you slice to keep the slices together). Starting in the
middle of the cake, fan each quarter over the batter to reach the edge.
Repeat with the remaining peach quarters to make a star-like pattern.

6. Drizzle the remaining 2 tablespoons honey over the peaches.

7. Bake for 38 to 42 minutes, until the peaches are tender and a toothpick
inserted in the middle comes out clean. Place the pan on a wire cooling
rack.

8. In a small microwave-safe bowl, melt the apricot fruit spread in the
microwave, or melt in a small saucepan over medium heat, then brush the
top of the hot cake. Let cool for 25 minutes. Remove the ring from the pan
and continue to let cool. Slice and serve warm or at room temperature.

9. The cake is best served the day it's made.

Chocolate Soufflé

A deceivingly simple recipe that produces a showstopping result. The Maple Whipped Cream is not to be missed. We recommend pairing with our Roasted Strawberries, for the final bow.

SERVES 6

1 tablespoon unsalted butter, for the soufflé dish

¼ cup (50 g) granulated sugar, plus more for the soufflé dish

7 large eggs, at cool room temperature

¾ cup (180 ml) heavy whipping cream

1¼ cups (213 g) dark chocolate chips

3 tablespoons Grand Marnier (optional)

⅛ teaspoon kosher salt

¼ teaspoon cream of tartar

1 recipe Maple Whipped Cream (page 236) and/or 1 recipe Roasted Strawberries (page 225)

1. Position an oven rack in the lower third of the oven. Preheat the oven to 425°F. Butter the bottom and up the sides to the rim of a deep 8-inch soufflé dish. Then coat the dish with sugar, tapping out any excess.

2. Separate the eggs. Put the 7 whites in the bowl of a stand mixer fitted with the whisk attachment, or in a large mixing bowl with a hand mixer, making sure there is no trace of egg yolks in the egg whites. Put 5 of the egg yolks in a small mixing bowl; reserve the other 2 yolks for another use.

3. In a small saucepan, heat the cream over medium heat until steaming. Remove from the heat and add the chocolate chips. Let stand for a few minutes, then whisk until melted and smooth. Whisk in the Grand Marnier (if using) and the salt. Then whisk in the egg yolks. Scrape the mixture into a large mixing bowl.

4. Add the cream of tartar to the egg whites. Using an electric mixer on medium-high speed, beat the egg whites until soft peaks form. With the mixer running, gradually pour in the sugar and beat until voluminous, stiff peaks form. This will take 2 to 4 minutes from start to finish.

5. One third at a time, use a silicone spatula to gently fold the egg whites into the chocolate mixture until no trace of white remains. Scrape the batter into the prepared dish. Do not level the top, as this will hinder a high rise. Slide into the oven and reduce the oven temperature to 375°F. Bake for 28 to 34 minutes, until puffed and cracked on top. (Do not open the oven door until 28 minutes have passed or you risk deflating the soufflé.) The center will be a little molten and gooey when you scoop into it.

6. Serve immediately with the Maple Whipped Cream or Roasted Strawberries, or both.

Sweet Potato Snacking Cake with Butterscotch Glaze

When this cake is on the counter, we quietly sliver off
bits all day long, hoping no one will notice. The maple syrup and
sweet potato combo makes it way too hard to resist.

SERVES 8

Cake

½ cup (120 g) roasted sweet potato, such
as Japanese sweet potato (We like it for
its light color)

2 large eggs

1 cup (237 g) whole milk

6 tablespoons (3 ounces; 84 g) unsalted
butter, melted

½ cup (120 ml) pure maple syrup

1 teaspoon pure vanilla extract

1¾ cups (259 g) gluten-free baking flour,
spooned and leveled

1 teaspoon baking soda

¾ teaspoon kosher salt

Glaze

2 tablespoons unsalted butter

¼ cup (46 g) coconut sugar

3 tablespoons pure maple syrup

3 tablespoons heavy whipping cream

1 teaspoon pure vanilla extract

¼ teaspoon kosher salt

1. Position an oven rack in the middle of the oven. Preheat the oven to
350°F. Spray an 8 × 8-inch square metal baking pan with cooking spray.
Line the bottom and up all four sides with parchment paper, leaving 1-inch
overhangs.

2. For the cake: In a food processor, puree the sweet potato until very
smooth. Mix in the eggs until well incorporated, scraping down the sides
with a silicone spatula as necessary. Add the milk, butter, maple syrup, and
vanilla and mix in.

3. In a large mixing bowl, whisk together the flour, baking soda, and salt.
Add the sweet potato mixture and whisk together until well combined.

4. Using a silicone spatula, scrape the batter into the prepared pan and
level the top.

5. Bake for 34 to 38 minutes, until a toothpick inserted in the middle comes
out with a few moist crumbs attached. Place the pan on a wire cooling rack
and let the cake cool to room temperature.

6. When the cake is cool, make the glaze: In a small saucepan, melt the
butter over medium heat. Whisk in the coconut sugar and maple syrup.
Continue whisking for about 30 seconds as the mixture bubbles and the
sugar melts. Whisk in the cream. Let it simmer for 1 to 2 minutes, whisking
often, until the sauce starts to thicken. Remove from the heat and whisk in
the vanilla and salt.

7. Let the sauce cool for about 10 minutes, stirring occasionally, so it
thickens but remains pourable. Drizzle the glaze over the cake and spread
evenly over the top. Let the glaze cool until set, about 15 minutes.

8. Grab the edges of the parchment and lift the cake onto a cutting board.
Slice into squares.

9. The cake will keep, tightly wrapped, at room temperature for up to
3 days.

Spice Cake with Whipped Apricot Frosting

Stewed apricots sweeten this frosting beautifully. A layer cake like this one would typically have 3 to 4 cups of white sugar. Ours has just a little more than 1 full cup of coconut sugar and date sugar combined, and it more than satisfies.

SERVES 8 TO 10

Nonstick vegetable oil cooking spray

Cake

3 cups (444 g) gluten-free baking flour, spooned and leveled

2/3 cup (130 g) coconut sugar

1/2 cup (72 g) date sugar

2 1/2 teaspoons ground cinnamon

1 1/4 teaspoons ground cloves

1/2 teaspoon finely grated nutmeg

2 teaspoons baking powder

1/2 teaspoon baking soda

1 teaspoon kosher salt

2 sticks (8 ounces; 226 g) unsalted butter, at room temperature

6 large egg yolks, at cool room temperature (use the egg whites for Chocolate–Hazelnut Meringue Cake, page 90)

1 1/2 cups (360 ml) buttermilk, at cool room temperature

2 teaspoons pure vanilla extract

Frosting

1 1/2 recipes (1 1/2 cups; 393 g) Apricot Puree (page 229)

1 cup (240 ml) heavy whipping cream

1/4 cup (56 g) mascarpone cheese

1. Position an oven rack in the middle of the oven. Preheat the oven to 350°F. Spray two 8-inch round metal cake pans with cooking spray. Line the bottoms with parchment paper.

2. For the cake: In the bowl of a stand mixer fitted with the paddle attachment, or a large mixing bowl with a hand mixer, whisk together the flour, coconut sugar, date sugar, cinnamon, cloves, nutmeg, baking powder, baking soda, and salt. Add the butter. Beat together on medium-low speed until the mixture resembles damp sand (and is without lumps).

3. In a small mixing bowl, whisk together the egg yolks, buttermilk, and vanilla. Add to the large bowl and beat on medium-low speed for 30 seconds, until combined and fluffy, scraping down the sides of the bowl with a silicone spatula as necessary.

4. Dividing evenly, scrape the batter into the prepared pans and level the tops. Bake for 28 to 32 minutes, until a toothpick inserted in the middle comes out with a few moist crumbs attached.

5. Place the pans on a wire cooling rack and let cool for 25 minutes. Run a paring knife around the edges of the cakes to loosen them from the pans. Invert the cakes onto the wire rack and remove the parchment paper. Flip the cakes back over and let them cool completely.

6. For the frosting: In the bowl of a stand mixer fitted with the whisk attachment, or a large mixing bowl with a hand mixer, combine 1 cup of the Apricot Puree, the cream, and the mascarpone cheese. Beat together on medium speed for about 1 minute, or until thick and spreadable.

7. To frost the cake, place one of the cakes on a serving plate or cake stand. Frost the top of the cake with about 3/4 cup (180 ml) of the frosting. Place the other cake on top. Frost the top and sides of the cake.

8. To garnish, spoon the remaining 1/2 cup Apricot Puree into a small pastry bag with a 1/4-inch tip. Or make your own bag: Spoon the mixture into a zip-top plastic bag and use scissors to cut a 1/4-inch hole in one of the corners. Pipe small dots over the top and sides of the cake. Slice and serve.

9. The frosted cake can be refrigerated for up to 2 days under a cake dome. Let the cake come to room temperature before serving. Any leftovers, tightly wrapped, will last even longer.

SPICE CAKE with WHIPPED APRICOT FROSTING / 78

Olive Oil Cake with Pine Nuts and Orange

Traditional olive oil cakes have about 1 cup of sugar.
We use ⅓ cup of honey and added pine nuts, raisins, and rum.
Enjoy any time of day, year-round.

SERVES 8

Nonstick vegetable oil cooking spray

¼ cup (35 g) pine nuts

1½ cups (162 g) super-fine almond flour, spooned and leveled

¾ cup (111 g) gluten-free baking flour, spooned and leveled

1 teaspoon baking powder

½ teaspoon baking soda

½ teaspoon kosher salt

2 large eggs

¾ cup (180 ml) extra virgin olive oil

⅓ cup (80 ml) honey

Finely grated zest of 1 navel orange

¼ cup (60 ml) fresh orange juice (from 1 navel orange)

¼ cup (60 ml) dark rum

1 teaspoon pure vanilla extract

½ cup (80 g) golden raisins, chopped

1. Position an oven rack in the middle of the oven. Preheat the oven to 350°F. Spray an 8-inch round metal cake pan with cooking spray. Line the bottom of the pan with parchment paper.

2. Spread the pine nuts on a small rimmed sheet pan. Bake for 6 to 8 minutes, shaking the pan halfway through, until golden brown. Let cool.

3. In a medium mixing bowl, whisk together the almond flour, baking flour, baking powder, baking soda, and salt until well combined and no almond flour lumps remain.

4. In a large mixing bowl, whisk together the eggs. Then whisk in the olive oil and honey until well combined. Add the orange zest, orange juice, rum, and vanilla and whisk in.

5. Add the dry ingredients to the wet ingredients and whisk until well incorporated.

6. Using a silicone spatula, stir in the raisins and pine nuts.

7. Scrape the batter into the prepared pan. Bake for 34 to 38 minutes, until springy to the touch and a toothpick comes out clean when inserted in the middle.

8. Place the pan on a wire cooling rack and let cool for 25 minutes. Run a paring knife around the cake to loosen it from the pan. Invert the cake onto the wire rack and remove the parchment paper. Flip the cake back over and let cool. Slice and serve.

9. The cake will keep, tightly wrapped, at room temperature for up to 4 days.

Pumpkin Loaf Cake with Maple Frosting

The perfect holiday loaf cake to impress your friends and family.

SERVES 8

Nonstick vegetable oil cooking spray

Cake

2 large eggs

1 cup (227 g) canned pure pumpkin puree

2/3 cup (160 ml) extra virgin olive oil

1/3 cup (80 ml) date syrup

1/3 cup (65 g) coconut sugar

1 teaspoon pure vanilla extract

2 teaspoons ground cinnamon, plus more for dusting

1 teaspoon ground cloves

1/4 teaspoon finely grated nutmeg

1 teaspoon kosher salt

2 cups (296 g) gluten-free baking flour, spooned and leveled

1 teaspoon baking powder

1/2 teaspoon baking soda

Frosting

6 ounces (171 g) block cream cheese, at cool room temperature

4 tablespoons (2 ounces; 57 g) unsalted butter, at cool room temperature

1/4 cup (60 ml) pure maple syrup

1. Position an oven rack in the middle of the oven. Preheat the oven to 350°F. Spray an 8½ x 4½-inch metal loaf pan with cooking spray. Line the bottom and up the two long sides with parchment paper, leaving 1-inch overhangs.

2. For the cake: In a large mixing bowl, whisk together the eggs. Add the pumpkin puree, olive oil, date syrup, coconut sugar, vanilla, cinnamon, cloves, nutmeg, and salt and whisk together. Add the flour, baking powder, and baking soda. Using a silicone spatula, stir in until well incorporated.

3. Scrape the batter into the prepared pan and level the top. Bake for 55 to 60 minutes, until a toothpick inserted in the middle comes out with a few moist crumbs attached. Place the pan on a wire cooling rack and let cool for 25 minutes. Grab the edges of the parchment and lift the cake onto the wire rack and let cool completely.

4. For the frosting: In the bowl of a stand mixer fitted with the whisk attachment, or in a large mixing bowl with a hand mixer, combine the cream cheese and butter. Beat together on medium-high speed, until smooth and fluffy. Add the maple syrup and beat in until well combined and creamy.

5. Place the cake on a serving plate. Frost the top and dust with a little cinnamon. Slice and serve.

6. The frosted cake can be refrigerated for up to 2 days under a cake dome. Let the cake come to room temperature before serving. Any leftovers, tightly wrapped, will last even longer.

Basque Cheesecake

Here, we've sneaked in a traditional, full-sugar favorite so you can choose which "lifestyle" is for you. This cheesecake is unbeatable with its burnt sugar top and creamy center. And, believe it or not, it's so easy: no crust and no water bath. Serve with Roasted Strawberries (page 225), Roasted Blueberries (page 234), or Cherry Compote (page 235).

SERVES 8 TO 10

Nonstick vegetable oil cooking spray

Four 8-ounce packages (908 g) block cream cheese, at cool room temperature

1½ cups (300 g) granulated sugar

6 large eggs, at cool room temperature

½ cup (120 ml) heavy whipping cream

½ cup (114 g) sour cream

2 tablespoons cornstarch

2 teaspoons pure vanilla extract

½ teaspoon kosher salt

1. Spray a 9-inch springform pan with cooking spray (this will help the parchment paper stick to the pan). Line the bottom and up the sides of the pan, pressing into the corners, with a large piece of parchment paper, leaving a 2-inch overhang all the way around the rim of the pan (you may need to use 2 pieces of parchment, depending on the width of your roll).

2. In the bowl of a stand mixer fitted with the paddle attachment, or in a large mixing bowl with a hand mixer, beat the cream cheese on medium-low speed until creamy and without lumps (you don't want it to be fluffy), scraping down the sides of the bowl with a silicone spatula as necessary. Mix in the sugar. Add the eggs one at a time, mixing for 20 seconds before adding the next, making sure to scrape down the sides.

3. In a small mixing bowl, whisk together the cream, sour cream, cornstarch, vanilla, and salt. Scrape this mixture into the cream cheese mixture and mix on medium-low speed until well incorporated.

4. Scrape the batter into the prepared pan. Refrigerate for at least 30 minutes and up to 1 hour.

5. Position an oven rack in the middle of the oven. Preheat the oven to 450°F.

6. Place the cheesecake on a large rimmed sheet pan and slide into the oven. Bake for 40 to 45 minutes, until the top is a deep golden brown, the edges are puffed and a little cracked, and the center is still a little wobbly. You do not want to overbake it. If in doubt, underbake.

7. Place the cheesecake on a wire cooling rack and let cool to room temperature, about 1½ hours. If you like a slightly warm, wobbly cheesecake, you can serve it at this point. Or, if you like it with a chill, refrigerate it for about 4 hours or overnight. This will give it more time to set up, making it a little easier to slice.

8. Unlatch the ring of the pan and remove it. Peel back the parchment from around the sides. To slice, dip a large chef's knife in hot water and wipe dry with each cut. Serve.

9. The cake will keep, tightly wrapped, in the refrigerator for up to 4 days.

Pineapple Upside-Down Coconut Cake

This cake tastes like a tropical vacation. It also has half the amount of sugar of typical upside-down cakes. You won't miss it with a bit of maple syrup in there.

SERVES 8

Nonstick vegetable oil cooking spray

Pineapple Topping

2 tablespoons unsalted butter or vegan butter

3 tablespoons coconut sugar

1 tablespoon pure maple syrup

Small pinch of kosher salt

1/3 of a small fresh, ripe pineapple, skin removed

Cake

3 large eggs

2/3 cup (160 ml) unsweetened coconut milk, well shaken or whisked

1/2 cup (120 ml) pure maple syrup

1/3 cup (74 g) coconut oil, melted

1/2 teaspoon pure vanilla extract

1½ cups (222 g) gluten-free baking flour, spooned and leveled

1½ teaspoons baking powder

1/4 teaspoon baking soda

1/2 teaspoon kosher salt

1. Position an oven rack in the middle of the oven. Preheat the oven to 350°F. Spray an 8-inch round metal cake pan with cooking spray.

2. For the pineapple topping: In a small saucepan, melt the butter over medium heat. Add the coconut sugar, maple syrup, and salt. Whisk together for about 1 minute, or until the coconut sugar melts and the mixture comes together to make a smooth caramel sauce. Immediately scrape it into the prepared pan and spread over the bottom.

3. Slice the pineapple into 1/4-inch-thick rounds. Then cut the rounds into bite-size triangles, avoiding the core. Arrange them over the caramel in a single layer, spacing closely together.

4. For the cake: In a medium mixing bowl, whisk together the eggs. Then whisk in the coconut milk, maple syrup, coconut oil, and vanilla.

5. In a small mixing bowl, whisk together the flour, baking powder, baking soda, and salt. Add to the wet ingredients and whisk until well incorporated.

6. Scrape the batter over the pineapple slices and level the top.

7. Bake for 40 to 45 minutes, until springy to the touch and a toothpick inserted in the middle comes out clean. Let cool on a wire cooling rack for 15 minutes. Run a paring knife around the edge of the cake to loosen it from the pan. Place a large serving plate over the cake pan and, holding them tightly together, quickly invert the two. Lift off the pan. If any of the pineapple sticks to the pan, use a small knife or offset spatula to replace it on the cake. Let the cake cool to room temperature. Slice and serve.

8. The cake is best served the day it's made.

Chocolate–Hazelnut Meringue Cake

As we tested this beauty, we decided it deserved to remain sugar-full. It's just so good. Light and creamy with crunchy layers—someone you love deserves this on a special occasion.

SERVES 6 TO 8

Meringue Layers

1 cup plus 2 tablespoons (160 g) roasted whole hazelnuts, skins removed

3/4 cup plus 2 tablespoons (175 g) granulated sugar

1/4 cup (36 g) roasted unsalted almonds

6 large egg whites (use the egg yolks for Spice Cake with Whipped Apricot Frosting, page 78)

1/4 teaspoon cream of tartar

1 tablespoon cornstarch

1/8 teaspoon kosher salt

Filling

13/4 cups (420 ml) heavy whipping cream

1/2 cup (128 g) dark chocolate chips

11/2 teaspoons pure vanilla extract

Block of dark chocolate, for shaving

1. Position two oven racks toward the middle of the oven. Preheat the oven to 325°F. Line two large rimmed sheet pans with parchment paper.

2. Next, make the outlines for the meringue layers. Draw five 9 × 5-inch rectangles on the two pieces of parchment paper. For ease, place an 8½ x 4½-inch metal loaf pan, top side down, on one of the parchment-lined sheet pans. Use a pen to trace around the loaf pan. Trace another rectangle. Flip the parchment over. Repeat this process on the other piece of parchment, but this time make 3 rectangles. Set aside.

3. For the meringue layers: In a food processor, grind 1 cup of the hazelnuts with 1 tablespoon of the sugar until they resemble coffee grounds. Pour into a small mixing bowl. Do the same with the almonds and 1 tablespoon of the sugar. Add to the bowl of hazelnuts.

4. In the bowl of a stand mixer fitted with the whisk attachment, or in a large mixing bowl with a hand mixer, beat the egg whites and cream of tartar on medium-high speed until foamy and white. Then, with the mixer running, gradually pour in the remaining 3/4 cup sugar (this should take about 1 minute). Continue to beat for 2 to 3 minutes more, until stiff, shiny, voluminous peaks form.

5. Add the ground almonds and hazelnuts, the cornstarch, and the salt to the meringue mixture. Using a silicone spatula, gently fold in until well combined. Scrape the mixture into a pastry bag with a 1/2-inch tip. Or make your own bag: Scrape the mixture into a zip-top plastic bag and use scissors to cut a 1/2-inch hole in one of the corners.

6. Pipe along the outlines of the prepared rectangle patterns, then fill them in by piping continuous lines about 1/2 inch high. Smooth the tops with an offset metal spatula or knife. The important thing is that all of the piped rectangles be the same size and thickness.

7. Bake for 25 to 30 minutes, rotating the pans 180° and switching them from top to bottom about halfway through, until the layers are light golden brown, firm around the edges, but still a little soft (not crisp) to the touch in the middle. Place the pans on a wire cooling rack and let cool completely. The layers will have a little bend to them and should peel easily from the parchment. If not, return them to the oven and bake for a few minutes more.

8. For the filling: In a small saucepan, heat 1/2 cup of the cream over medium heat until steaming. Remove from the heat and add the chocolate chips. Let stand for a few minutes, then whisk until melted and smooth. Whisk in the vanilla. Let cool to room temperature (it should still be pourable).

9. In the bowl of a stand mixer fitted with the whisk attachment, or in a large mixing bowl with a hand mixer, beat the remaining 1 1/4 cups cream on medium speed until soft peaks form. Pour in the chocolate mixture and beat until medium-stiff peaks form.

10. To assemble, place a meringue layer on a serving plate and spread a thin layer of filling (about 2/3 cup) over the top. Top with another meringue and more filling. Repeat to form 5 layers of meringue ending with the final meringue layer topped with filling.

11. Coarsely chop the remaining 2 tablespoons hazelnuts and scatter them over the top of the cake.

12. Using a vegetable peeler, shave thin curls from the block of chocolate over the cake. Refrigerate for at least 3 hours to let it set. Slice and serve.

13. The cake can be refrigerated for up to 2 days under a cake dome. Any leftovers, wrapped tightly, will last even longer.

CHOCOLATE–
HAZELNUT
MERINGUE CAKE
90

Blackberry Buckle

I got a little tired of berry crisp, so I thought it was time to include a buckle, a cake loaded with fruit. Sweetened with blackberries and maple syrup and topped with a dusting of cinnamon, this is a good one, especially if you are grain-free.

SERVES 8

Nonstick vegetable oil cooking spray

6 tablespoons (3 ounces; 84 g) unsalted butter

3 large eggs

½ cup (114 g) sour cream

⅓ cup (80 ml) pure maple syrup

1 teaspoon pure vanilla extract

1½ cups (162 g) super-fine almond flour, spooned and leveled

½ teaspoon baking powder

½ teaspoon kosher salt

½ teaspoon finely grated nutmeg

3 cups (432 g) fresh blackberries

1 tablespoon coconut sugar, for sprinkling

½ teaspoon ground cinnamon, for sprinkling

1. Position an oven rack in the middle of the oven. Preheat the oven to 375°F. Spray an 8-inch square metal baking pan with cooking spray. Line the bottom and up two opposite sides with parchment paper, leaving 1-inch overhangs.

2. In a small skillet, melt the butter over medium heat. Once the butter is melted, swirl the pan for 3 to 4 minutes, until the little milk solids at the bottom of the pan turn golden brown (keep a close eye on them as they can burn quickly). Immediately scrape the browned butter into a small bowl and let cool to room temperature.

3. In a medium mixing bowl, whisk together the eggs. Add the sour cream, maple syrup, and vanilla and whisk together. Whisk in the browned butter.

4. In a small mixing bowl, whisk together the almond flour, baking powder, salt, and nutmeg, making sure no lumps of almond flour remain. Add to the wet ingredients and whisk until well incorporated.

5. Using a silicone spatula, gently fold the blackberries into the batter. Scrape the batter into the prepared pan and spread evenly over the bottom. Sprinkle the top with the coconut sugar and cinnamon.

6. Bake for 28 to 32 minutes, until a toothpick inserted in the middle comes out clean. Place the pan on a wire cooling rack and let cool to room temperature. Grab the edges of the parchment and lift the buckle onto a cutting board. Slice and serve.

7. The buckle is best served the day it's made.

Chocolate Cupcakes

These cupcakes are moist, rich, and delicious. When
I fed them to my kids, they devoured them, not noticing there
is half the sugar than in other ones I used to make. That's
when I realized we were eating too much sugar.

MAKES 12 CUPCAKES

Cupcakes

1½ cups (222 g) gluten-free baking flour, spooned and leveled

½ cup (92 g) coconut sugar

⅓ cup (28 g) unsweetened cocoa powder, spooned and leveled

¾ teaspoon baking soda

½ teaspoon kosher salt

1 cup plus 2 tablespoons (270 ml) plant-based milk, such as oat, almond, or cashew

½ cup (120 ml) extra virgin olive oil

1½ teaspoons pure vanilla extract

Frosting

⅓ cup (80 ml) unsweetened coconut cream, well shaken or whisked

½ cup (86 g) dark chocolate chips (vegan, if desired)

1 teaspoon pure vanilla extract

⅛ teaspoon kosher salt

1. Position an oven rack in the middle of the oven. Preheat the oven to 350°F. Line a 12-cup muffin pan with paper liners.

2. For the cupcakes: In a large mixing bowl, whisk together the flour, coconut sugar, cocoa powder, baking soda, and salt.

3. Add the milk, olive oil, and vanilla and whisk together until well incorporated. Divide the batter evenly into the prepared muffin pan, filling each cup about half full. Use the back of a spoon to level the tops.

4. Bake for 18 to 22 minutes, until puffed and springy to the touch. Let cool completely on a wire cooling rack, then take the cupcakes out and place on the rack.

5. For the frosting: In a small saucepan, heat the coconut cream over medium heat until steaming. Remove from the heat and add the chocolate chips. Let stand for a few minutes, then whisk until melted and smooth. Stir in the vanilla and salt.

6. Let the frosting cool for a few minutes so it thickens to honey consistency. Then spoon a scant tablespoon of the frosting onto each cupcake, letting it spread over the tops. Let the frosting cool for about 30 minutes, or until set, before serving.

7. Store the cupcakes in an airtight container for up to 4 days.

Walnut Crumb Coffee Cake

We loaded up the crumb and minimized the cake. If you make it for brunch, it will be gone by supper.

SERVES 8

Nonstick vegetable oil cooking spray

Walnut Crumb

½ cup (74 g) gluten-free baking flour, spooned and leveled

¼ cup (46 g) coconut sugar

½ teaspoon ground cinnamon

¼ teaspoon kosher salt

4 tablespoons (2 ounces; 57 g) cold unsalted butter, cut into small pieces

½ cup (64 g) walnuts, coarsely chopped

Cake

¾ cup (111 g) gluten-free baking flour, spooned and leveled

¾ cup (81 g) super-fine almond flour, spooned and leveled

¾ teaspoon ground cardamom or ½ teaspoon finely grated nutmeg

1 teaspoon baking powder

¼ teaspoon baking soda

¼ teaspoon kosher salt

2 large eggs

½ cup (114 g) sour cream

⅓ cup (80 ml) pure maple syrup

4 tablespoons (2 ounces; 57 g) unsalted butter, melted

1 teaspoon pure vanilla extract

1. Position an oven rack in the middle of the oven. Preheat the oven to 350°F. Spray a 9-inch springform pan with cooking spray.

2. For the walnut crumb: In a small mixing bowl, whisk together the flour, coconut sugar, cinnamon, and salt. Add the butter. Using your fingertips, combine the butter with the dry ingredients until evenly incorporated and moist crumbs form. Mix in the walnuts. Refrigerate.

3. For the cake: In a small mixing bowl, whisk together the baking flour, almond flour, cardamom, baking powder, baking soda, and salt until well incorporated and no almond flour lumps remain.

4. In a large mixing bowl, whisk together the eggs. Add the sour cream, maple syrup, butter, and vanilla and whisk together. Add the dry ingredients and whisk until well combined.

5. Scrape the batter into the prepared pan and level the top. Scatter the walnut crumb over the top of the batter, squeezing it into small clumps as you go.

6. Bake for 28 to 32 minutes, until a toothpick inserted in the middle comes out clean. Place the pan on a wire cooling rack and let cool for 25 minutes before removing the ring. Serve slightly warm or at room temperature.

7. The cake will keep, tightly wrapped, at room temperature for up to 4 days.

Carrot Cake with Pineapple Whipped Cream

Applesauce, raisins, and carrots do most of the sweetening here. I don't know how I've eaten it any other way. All the sugar in traditional recipes is now a thing of the past.

SERVES 8

Nonstick vegetable oil cooking spray

Cake

1/2 cup (64 g) walnuts

1 cup (160 g) golden raisins

About 2 cups boiling water, for plumping the raisins

2 medium carrots, peeled and quartered crosswise

2 large eggs

1/2 cup (128 g) unsweetened applesauce

1/4 cup (60 ml) pure maple syrup

1/4 cup (60 ml) extra virgin olive oil

1 teaspoon pure vanilla extract

2 cups (216 g) super-fine almond flour, spooned and leveled

2 teaspoons ground cinnamon

1 teaspoon baking soda

1/2 teaspoon kosher salt

1/2 cup (40 g) unsweetened shredded coconut

Frosting

2 ounces (57 g) block cream cheese, at cool room temperature

3/4 cup (180 ml) heavy whipping cream

6 tablespoons (120 g) pineapple-mango fruit spread

Unsweetened toasted coconut flakes, for topping

Fresh blueberries, for topping

1. Position an oven rack in the middle of the oven. Preheat the oven to 350°F. Spray a 9-inch round metal cake pan with cooking spray and line the bottom with parchment paper.

2. For the cake: Spread the walnuts on a small rimmed sheet pan. Bake for 8 to 10 minutes, until fragrant and crisp. Once cool, finely chop them.

3. Put the raisins in a small mixing bowl. Add the boiling water to cover them by 1 inch and let stand for 10 minutes, or until very soft. Place a strainer over a bowl; drain the raisins into the strainer, reserving the liquid.

4. Put the raisins, carrots, and 1 tablespoon of the reserved raisin liquid in a food processor and puree until very smooth. Add a little more of the reserved raisin liquid, if necessary, to help smooth out the mixture.

5. In a large mixing bowl, whisk the eggs. Add the applesauce, maple syrup, olive oil, vanilla, and the carrot-raisin puree and whisk together. Add the almond flour, cinnamon, baking soda, and salt and whisk together, making sure no almond flour lumps remain. Using a silicone spatula, stir in the shredded coconut and walnuts.

6. Scrape the batter into the prepared pan and level the top. Bake for 38 to 45 minutes, until a toothpick inserted in the middle comes out clean. Place the pan on a wire cooling rack and let cool for 25 minutes. Run a paring knife around the edges of the cake to loosen it from the pan. Invert the cake onto the wire rack and remove the parchment paper. Flip the cake back over and let it cool completely.

7. For the frosting: In the bowl of a stand mixer fitted with the whisk attachment, or in a large mixing bowl with a hand mixer, beat the cream cheese on medium speed until fluffy and smooth. Add the cream and fruit spread and beat until soft peaks form.

8. Place the cake on a serving plate and frost the top of the cake. Top with coconut flakes and blueberries. Slice and serve.

9. Refrigerate leftovers, tightly wrapped, for up to 4 days.

Sticky Date Cake with Rum Caramel Sauce

Maple syrup and dates make this cake a welcome treat at
the end of a meal. The caramel sauce is fantastic over the ice cream,
but we use it many ways in this book.

SERVES 8

Nonstick vegetable oil cooking spray

Cake

11 Medjool dates (242 g), pitted

1 teaspoon baking soda

1 cup (240 ml) boiling water

⅓ cup (80 ml) pure maple syrup

1 teaspoon pure vanilla extract

1 large egg

1 cup (148 g) gluten-free baking flour,
spooned and leveled

1½ teaspoons baking powder

½ teaspoon kosher salt

Rum Caramel Sauce

1 recipe Oat Milk Caramel (page 224)

1 tablespoon dark rum or bourbon

Vanilla ice cream, for serving (dairy-free, if
desired)

1. Position an oven rack in the middle of the oven. Preheat the oven to 350°F. Spray an 8-inch square metal baking pan with cooking spray. Line the bottom and up two opposite sides with parchment paper, leaving 1-inch overhangs.

2. For the cake: Put the dates and baking soda in a food processor. Add the boiling water and let stand for 10 minutes, or until very soft. (Make sure all of the dates are submerged in the water.)

3. Puree the date mixture until very smooth, scraping down the sides with a silicone spatula as necessary. Mix in the maple syrup and vanilla. Make sure this mixture is cooled to room temperature before blending in the egg (you don't want to scramble it). Add the flour, baking powder, and salt and pulse several times until well incorporated.

4. Using a silicone spatula, scrape the batter into the prepared pan and level the top. Bake until a toothpick inserted in the middle comes out with a few moist crumbs attached, 28 to 34 minutes. Let cool on a wire cooling rack for 25 minutes. Grab the edges of the parchment and lift the cake onto the wire rack and let cool to room temperature.

5. For the rum caramel sauce: Warm the Oat Milk Caramel and stir in the rum.

6. To serve, slice the cake and divide among plates. Top with a small scoop of ice cream and drizzle with the rum caramel sauce.

7. The cake will keep, tightly wrapped, at room temperature for up to 4 days.

Strawberry Crepe Cake

This one requires some time and effort, but the results
are showstopping. Sweetened with only 1/3 cup of honey, this
recipe will leave your friends and family awestruck.

SERVES 8

Crepes

3 large eggs

1 1/3 cups (320 ml) whole milk, oat milk, or
cashew milk

1 cup (148 g) gluten-free baking flour,
spooned and leveled

1/4 teaspoon kosher salt

1 1/2 teaspoons pure vanilla extract

3 tablespoons unsalted butter, melted,
plus more for cooking

Filling

1 1/3 cups (26 g) freeze-dried strawberries

2 cups (480 ml) heavy whipping cream

1/3 cup (80 ml) honey

1 pint (12 ounces; 340 g) fresh medium-
size strawberries, thinly sliced

1. For the crepes: In a large mixing bowl, whisk together the eggs, then whisk in 1/3 cup of the milk. Add the flour and salt and whisk until no lumps remain. Gradually whisk in the remaining 1 cup milk. Whisk in the vanilla and melted butter. Let stand for 10 minutes.

2. Place an 8-inch nonstick skillet over medium heat. Once it's hot, add a tiny amount of butter and swirl the skillet to coat the bottom. Measure a scant 1/4 cup (60 ml) of the batter and pour into the skillet. Quickly swirl the skillet to make a thin pancake that covers the bottom of the skillet. Cook for 1 to 1 1/2 minutes, until the underside has golden brown streaks. Flip the crepe and cook for 30 seconds more. Slide it onto a large plate and repeat with the remaining batter. (Turn down the heat if the skillet starts to get too hot.) You should get 12 crepes total. Refrigerate the crepes until completely cool.

3. For the filling: Finely grind the freeze-dried strawberries: Put them in a zip-top plastic bag, squeeze out the air, and seal. Use a rolling pin to finely grind them to a powder. (Alternatively, you can use a food processor or blender.)

4. In the bowl of a stand mixer fitted with the whisk attachment, or in a large mixing bowl with a hand mixer, beat the cream on medium speed until soft peaks form. Beat in the freeze-dried strawberry powder and the honey, scraping down the sides of the bowl as necessary, until thick and spreadable.

5. To assemble the cake, place 1 crepe on a serving plate and evenly spread a thin layer of the filling (about 1/4 cup; 60 ml) over the top and all the way to the edge. Layer with the remaining crepes and filling, ending with the final crepe topped with the filling.

6. Arrange the fresh strawberries in concentric circles over the top of the cake, starting from the outside and working your way in. Refrigerate for at least 1 hour, or until completely set. Slice and serve.

7. The frosted cake can be refrigerated for up to 2 days under a cake dome, but it's best to add the strawberries right before serving. Any leftovers, tightly wrapped, will keep even longer.

STRAWBERRY CREPE CAKE / 105

Pies & Pastries

Roasted Strawberry Pop Tarts
(Frosted/Unfrosted)

Our family knows a thing or two about Pop-Tarts. And this version is so good! You get to decide if you frost them or not. Frosting obviously adds a lot more sugar, but you've already done wonders by making your own with wholesome ingredients rather than buying them from the store.

MAKES 6

Pastry

1½ cups (180 g) all-purpose flour, spooned and leveled, plus more for rolling

½ cup (54 g) super-fine almond flour, spooned and leveled

1 tablespoon coconut sugar

½ teaspoon kosher salt

1½ sticks (12 tablespoons; 6 ounces; 168 g) cold unsalted butter or vegan butter, cut into small pieces

4 to 5 tablespoons ice water

1 teaspoon pure vanilla extract

Filling

1½ pounds fresh strawberries (2 pints; 681 g), hulled and quartered

3 tablespoons maple syrup

Icing (optional)

5 teaspoons reserved strawberry liquid

1¼ cups (145 g) confectioners' sugar

1 teaspoon pure vanilla extract

1½ teaspoons fresh lemon juice

Small pinch of kosher salt

1. For the pastry: In a food processor, combine the all-purpose flour, almond flour, coconut sugar, and salt. Pulse a couple of times to combine. Add the butter pieces and pulse several times until the butter pieces are pea-size. Add 4 tablespoons of the ice water and the vanilla. Pulse until moist crumbs form and the dough holds together when pinched. If it's a little dry, add the remaining 1 tablespoon water.

2. On a large piece of plastic wrap, pour out the crumbs and gather them into a large ball. Knead a couple of times to bring the dough together. Divide the dough in half and shape into two ½-inch-thick rectangles. Wrap each one tightly in plastic wrap and refrigerate for at least 30 minutes or up to 1 day.

3. While the pastry dough rests, make the filling: In a medium saucepan, stir together the strawberries and maple syrup. Place over medium-high heat and let come to a boil. Reduce the heat to medium and simmer, stirring occasionally, for 10 minutes. Then scoop out 5 teaspoons of the strawberry liquid into a small bowl and set it aside for the icing. Continue to simmer the strawberries for 5 to 10 minutes more, until they break down and thicken into a jam. Let cool to room temperature, then refrigerate until ready to use.

4. Let the cold dough rest at room temperature for about 15 minutes, or until pliable for easy rolling.

5. Position an oven rack in the middle of the oven. Preheat the oven to 375°F. Line a sheet pan with parchment paper.

6. On a lightly floured surface, roll out one piece of the dough into a long rectangle about 15 × 5 inches and 1/8 inch thick. Trim away any shaggy edges. Dividing evenly, cut crosswise into 6 rectangles (each about 2 1/2 inches wide). Place on the prepared pan and refrigerate while you roll out and cut the other piece of dough in the same fashion.

7. Spread about 1 1/2 tablespoons of the strawberry jam over the 6 chilled dough rectangles, leaving a 1/2-inch border. Top with the remaining 6 dough rectangles. Seal the edges first with your fingertips, then press together with the tines of a fork. Poke tiny steam holes on the tops with the tines of the fork. Refrigerate for 15 minutes.

8. Bake for 25 to 30 minutes, until golden brown around the edges. Place the pan on a wire cooling rack and let cool completely.

9. Make the icing, if desired: To the small bowl containing the strawberry liquid, add the confectioners' sugar, vanilla, lemon juice, and salt and whisk together.

10. Frost the tops of the pop tarts and let the icing set, about 10 minutes, before serving.

11. These are best served the day they are made but will last well in an airtight container at room temperature for up to 4 days .

ROASTED STRAWBERRY POP TARTS / 110

Blueberry Galette

I always keep a bag of frozen blueberries in my freezer. I use them all the time for breakfast recipes and desserts like this one because they are so good for you. The apricot fruit spread is the only added sugar here, and we bake it in a flaky gluten-free crust.

SERVES 8

1 recipe Gluten-Free Pie Dough (page 226) or 1 recipe All-Purpose Pie Dough (page 227)

Gluten-free baking flour or all-purpose flour, for rolling

3 cups (432 g) fresh or frozen blueberries

¼ cup (80 g) apricot fruit spread

¼ teaspoon finely grated nutmeg

¼ teaspoon kosher salt

1 large egg, beaten, for brushing (optional)

1. Position an oven rack in the middle of the oven. Preheat the oven to 400°F.

2. Let the cold dough rest at room temperature for about 15 minutes, or until pliable for easy rolling.

3. Lightly flour a piece of parchment that's large enough to line a large rimmed sheet pan. Using a rolling pin, roll the dough into a 12-inch round that's about ⅛ inch thick, adding more flour as necessary to prevent sticking on top and underneath. Slide the parchment with the dough onto the sheet pan.

4. In a large bowl, toss together the blueberries, fruit spread, nutmeg, and salt.

5. Spread the berries over the dough, leaving a 2-inch border. Gently fold a section of the dough up and over the fruit. Continue to fold and pleat the dough as you go around to completely enclose the fruit. The dough cracks easily; just press it back together to mend. Refrigerate for 15 minutes.

6. Brush the crust with the beaten egg (if using).

7. Bake for 20 minutes at 400°F, then reduce the oven temperature to 375°F and bake for 25 to 30 minutes more, until the fruit is bubbling and the crust is golden brown and set. Place the pan on a wire cooling rack and let the galette cool to room temperature. Slice and serve.

8. The galette is best served the day it's made.

Strawberry Brown Butter Crostata

It looks fancy, but it's a simple, rustic dessert. No rolling out crust; instead, you make a very easy dough and press it into the pan. The strawberry, lemon, and brown butter flavors melded together are irresistible.

SERVES 8

1½ pounds (2 pints; 681 g) fresh strawberries, hulled and quartered

3 tablespoons maple syrup

1½ sticks (12 tablespoons; 6 ounces; 168 g) unsalted butter

1¾ cups plus 2 tablespoons (277 g) gluten-free baking flour

¼ cup (46 g) coconut sugar

1 teaspoon finely grated lemon zest

1 teaspoon baking powder

½ teaspoon kosher salt

1 large egg

1 teaspoon pure vanilla extract

1. In a medium saucepan, stir together the strawberries and maple syrup. Place over medium-high heat and let come to a boil. Reduce the heat to medium and simmer, stirring occasionally, for 15 to 20 minutes, until the mixture thickens into a jam. Let cool.

2. In a medium skillet, melt the butter over medium heat. Once the butter is melted, swirl the pan for 3 to 4 minutes, until the little milk solids at the bottom of the pan turn golden brown. Scrape the browned butter into a small bowl and let cool to room temperature.

3. In a large mixing bowl, whisk together the flour, coconut sugar, lemon zest, baking powder, and salt. Drizzle in the browned butter and stir to combine.

4. In small mixing bowl, beat together the egg and vanilla. Pour over the brown butter mixture and stir until well incorporated. Shape the dough into a rectangle. Cut off one third of the dough, wrap in plastic, and refrigerate for 20 minutes.

5. Position an oven rack in the middle of the oven. Preheat the oven to 350°F.

6. Press the remaining portion of dough evenly over the bottom and ¼ inch up the sides of a 9-inch tart pan with a removable bottom or a 9-inch springform pan. Refrigerate for 10 minutes.

7. Spread the strawberry jam evenly over the pressed-in crust.

8. Cut the remaining piece of dough evenly into 4 equal portions. Between the palms of your hands, roll each portion into a ball until pliable. Then, on a clean work surface, use your fingertips to roll (or pinch) each ball into a thin cord 9 inches long. Gently flatten the cords.

9. Lay the cords in a crosshatch pattern over the jam. (If the cords break, don't worry, just pinch them back together.) Gently press the ends into the outside crust.

10. Bake for 25 to 30 minutes, until the crust is light golden brown around the edges. Place the pan on a wire cooling rack and let cool completely. Unmold and slice. This is best served the day it's made.

Banana Cream Pie

We roast ripe bananas to help sweeten this winner.
The crust is a quick press-in and gluten-free. The filling tastes
like your favorite banana cream pie, with only a fraction
of the sugar (maple syrup does the job here).

SERVES 8

1 recipe Gluten-Free Pie Dough (page 226)

Pudding

3 very ripe medium-size bananas

1½ cups (360 ml) whole milk

¼ cup (60 ml) pure maple syrup

¼ teaspoon kosher salt

3 egg yolks

3 tablespoons cornstarch

2 tablespoons unsalted butter

1 teaspoon pure vanilla extract

1 tablespoon dark rum (optional)

2 perfectly ripe medium-size bananas

1 recipe Maple Whipped Cream
(page 236)

Block of dark chocolate, for shaving

1. Position an oven rack in the middle of the oven. Preheat the oven to 350°F.

2. Evenly press the pie dough over the bottom and about 2 inches up the sides of a 9-inch springform pan, making sure to press into the corners. Refrigerate for 15 minutes.

3. Bake the crust for 23 to 28 minutes, until light golden brown. Place the pan on a wire cooling rack and let cool to room temperature.

4. Meanwhile, make the pudding: Put the 3 very ripe (unpeeled) bananas on a small rimmed sheet pan. Bake for 20 to 25 minutes, until the bananas start to split and bubble a little.

5. Once the bananas are cool enough to handle, peel and put them in a blender or food processor, along with any residual juices left in the pan. Puree the bananas until very smooth, scraping down the sides as necessary. Add the milk, maple syrup, and salt and mix until well combined.

6. In a small saucepan, whisk together the egg yolks and cornstarch. Gradually whisk in ½ cup (120 ml) of the banana-milk mixture until smooth and without lumps, then whisk in the remaining mixture.

7. Place the saucepan over medium heat. Whisk occasionally for the first 2 minutes while the mixture heats up. Then whisk continuously, making sure to whisk the corners of the pan. It will first release steam, then once you see the first bubble, it will start to thicken. Continue to whisk for 1 minute more, until thickened to a pudding consistency. Remove from the heat. Whisk in the butter, vanilla, and rum (if using). This should take about 10 minutes from start to finish.

8. Scrape the pudding into the prepared pie shell and level the top. Refrigerate for at least 3 hours or overnight, until the pudding is set.

9. When ready to serve, thinly slice the 2 perfectly ripe bananas and lay them over the top of the pudding, starting from the outside and working your way toward the center.

10. Top the pie with the Maple Whipped Cream. Using a vegetable peeler, shave off curls from the block of chocolate directly over the whipped cream. Slice and serve. The pie can be refrigerated for up to 3 days.

Apple Tarts

These tarts are sweetened by pureed raisins and a little maple syrup and fruit spread. The puff pastry is store-bought, which makes life much easier. We are crazy about these in our house.

MAKES 6

Apple Ginger Puree

2 apples, such as Honey Crisp

1/2 cup (80 g) golden raisins

1/2 cup (120 ml) water, plus more if necessary

1/8 teaspoon kosher salt

2 teaspoons finely grated peeled fresh ginger

Tarts

1 or 2 sheets store-bought frozen puff pastry, vegan if desired, thawed

2 apples, such as Honey Crisp

Pinch of ground cinnamon

6 teaspoons pure maple syrup

2 tablespoons apricot fruit spread

1. For the apple ginger puree: Peel, core, and cut the apples into 1/2-inch dice. Put them in a medium saucepan. Add the raisins, water, and salt and cover with a tight-fitting lid. Place over medium-high heat and let come to a boil. Reduce the heat to medium-low and cook for 15 to 25 minutes, stirring occasionally, until the apples have broken down completely and no liquid remains. If the liquid cooks away before the apples are tender, add a little more water. Remove from the heat and add the ginger. Let cool.

2. Using a handheld or regular blender, puree the apple mixture until very smooth.

3. For the tarts: Position an oven rack in the middle of the oven. Preheat the oven to 400°F. Line a large rimmed sheet pan with parchment paper.

4. Roll out the puff pastry to 1/4 inch thick. Cut out six 41/2-inch rounds and place them on the prepared pan. (Depending on the size of the puff pastry sheets, you may need to roll out another sheet.) Spread about 2 tablespoons of the puree onto each round, leaving a 1/4-inch border.

5. Peel the apples. Cut them in half and scoop out the cores. Slice the apples very thin (about 1/16 inch). Dividing evenly, arrange the apples over the prepared puff pastry rounds, working your way around the edges, then toward the center, overlapping as you go. Sprinkle the tops with a little cinnamon. Drizzle 1 teaspoon maple syrup over each tart.

6. Bake for 35 to 40 minutes, until the puff pastry is puffed and golden brown and the apples are tender. To give the tarts a shine, heat the apricot fruit spread in the microwave or in a small saucepan over medium heat, then brush the tops. Serve warm or at room temperature.

7. These are best served the day they are made but will last well, tightly wrapped, at room temperature for up to 2 days.

Rosemary Shortcakes with Roasted Strawberries

Raisins act as our sweetener here, so if you don't like those,
I'd skip this recipe. Those who do will love the flavors of strawberry
and rosemary coming together.

SERVES 8

¾ cup (120 g) golden raisins, coarsely chopped

2 cups (296 g) gluten-free baking flour, spooned and leveled, plus more for the work surface

1 tablespoon baking powder

½ teaspoon kosher salt

1 stick (8 tablespoons; 4 ounces; 113 g) cold unsalted butter, cut into small pieces

½ cup (120 ml) heavy whipping cream, plus 1 to 2 tablespoons, if necessary, plus more for the tops

2 teaspoons finely chopped fresh rosemary

1 recipe Roasted Strawberries (page 225)

1 recipe Maple Whipped Cream (page 236)

1. Position an oven rack in the middle of the oven. Preheat the oven to 400°F. Line a large rimmed sheet pan with parchment paper.

2. Put the chopped raisins in a small mixing bowl and cover with very hot tap water to soften. Let them stand while you prep the shortcakes.

3. In a large bowl, whisk together the flour, baking powder, and salt. Add the butter. Using a pastry cutter or your fingertips, quickly cut the butter into the flour mixture until the pieces are the size of peas. Using a fork, stir in ½ cup of the cream. The mixture should resemble moist crumbs and hold together when pinched. If it's a little dry, stir in another 1 to 2 tablespoons of the remaining cream.

4. Drain the raisins in a strainer and shake out excess water. Stir the raisins and rosemary into the dough.

5. Using your hands, gather up the dough and shape it into a ball. Then, on a lightly floured work surface, press it into a 1-inch-thick disk. Cut into 8 triangles and place them on the prepared pan. Refrigerate for 10 minutes.

6. Brush the tops with a little cream. Bake for 18 to 22 minutes, until golden brown around the edges. Place the pan on a wire cooling rack and let cool completely.

7. Serve each shortcake with a large spoonful of the Roasted Strawberries and add a dollop of the Maple Whipped Cream.

8. The shortcakes will keep, tightly wrapped, at room temperature for up to 2 days. Warm them in the oven to freshen them up before serving.

Sweet Potato Coconut Rum Tart

The press-in pecan crust saves you time, while the luscious filling made with sweet potato, coconut, and cozy spices rivals any traditional pumpkin pie.

SERVES 8

Filling

2 medium sweet potatoes, such as garnet yam

1¼ cups (300 ml) coconut milk, well shaken or whisked

½ cup (120 ml) pure maple syrup

2 tablespoons dark rum (optional)

1 teaspoon pure vanilla extract

¾ teaspoon ground cinnamon

¾ teaspoon ground ginger

¼ teaspoon ground cloves

⅛ teaspoon finely grated nutmeg

¼ teaspoon kosher salt

3 large eggs

Crust

1½ cups (222 g) gluten-free baking flour, spooned and leveled

¾ cup (84 g) pecans

1 tablespoon coconut sugar

¼ teaspoon kosher salt

10 tablespoons (5 ounces; 140 g) cold unsalted butter or vegan butter, cut into small pieces

1 to 2 tablespoons ice water

1 recipe Maple Whipped Cream (page 236; optional)

1. Position an oven rack in the middle of the oven. Preheat the oven to 400°F.

2. For the filling: Place the potatoes on a small rimmed sheet pan and pierce a few times with a fork. Bake for 40 to 50 minutes, until very tender. Let cool.

3. Reduce the oven temperature to 350°F.

4. Meanwhile, make the crust: In a food processor, combine the flour, pecans, coconut sugar, and salt. Pulse until the pecans are finely chopped. Add the butter pieces and pulse until crumbly. Add 1 tablespoon of the water and pulse several times until large moist crumbs form. If it seems a little dry, add the remaining 1 tablespoon water.

5. Scatter the crumbs over the bottom of a 10-inch tart pan with a removable bottom. Press the crumbs evenly up the sides, then over the bottom of the pan, making sure to press the dough into the corners. Refrigerate for 15 minutes.

6. Place the tart pan on a large rimmed sheet pan. Bake for 25 to 35 minutes, until light golden brown. Place the pan on a wire cooling rack and let cool.

7. Back to the filling: Scoop out the flesh of the sweet potatoes and measure 1½ cups (360 g; save any remaining sweet potato for another use). Put in a food processor and puree until very smooth. Add the coconut milk, maple syrup, rum (if using), vanilla, cinnamon, ginger, cloves, nutmeg, and salt and pulse to combine, scraping down the sides as necessary with a silicone spatula. Add the eggs and pulse several times until well incorporated.

8. Pour the filling into the tart shell. Bake for 28 to 32 minutes, until the filling is set. Let cool completely before serving or refrigerate and serve chilled.

9. Slice and serve topped with the Maple Whipped Cream (if using). The pie can be refrigerated for up to 3 days.

Frangipane Galettes with Any Fruit

Frangipane is an almond custard used as a filling in tarts and galettes and is typically very sugary. We use our Apricot Puree to sweeten. You can top these galettes with whatever fruit is in season. This almondy-sweet, very pretty treat is a good weekend endeavor.

SERVES 6

Frangipane

½ cup (131 g) Apricot Puree (page 229)

4 tablespoons (2 ounces; 57 g) unsalted butter, at room temperature

1 large egg

1 tablespoon maple syrup

1 teaspoon pure almond extract

½ cup (54 g) super-fine almond flour

1 tablespoon cornstarch

½ teaspoon kosher salt

1 recipe All-Purpose Pie Dough (page 227) or 1 recipe Gluten-Free Pie Dough (page 226)

All-purpose flour or gluten-free baking flour, for rolling

Ripe fruit, such as apricots, figs, or oranges, cut into wedges, halves, or segments

¼ cup (80 g) apricot fruit spread

1. For the frangipane: In a food processor, combine the Apricot Puree and butter and beat until fluffy. Add the egg, maple syrup, and almond extract and mix in until well combined, scraping down the sides as necessary. Add the almond flour, cornstarch, and salt. Pulse several times until well incorporated. Scrape the frangipane into a bowl.

2. Position an oven rack in the middle of the oven. Preheat the oven to 375°F. Line a large rimmed sheet pan with parchment paper.

3. Let the cold pie dough rest at room temperature for about 15 minutes, or until pliable for easy rolling.

4. On a lightly floured surface, roll the dough into a 12-inch round that's about ⅛ inch thick, adding more flour as necessary to prevent sticking on top and underneath. Cut out six rounds about 5 inches across and place them on the prepared pan, rerolling the scraps as necessary. (Use a large round cookie cutter, or use a sharp paring knife to cut around the outside of a round plastic pint container lid.)

5. Spoon 3 tablespoons of the frangipane onto each round and spread evenly, leaving a 1-inch border. Arrange the fruit on the frangipane.

6. Crimp the pastry edges up and around the filling. The crimping doesn't have to be perfect; it just needs to hold in the frangipane. Refrigerate the galettes for 15 minutes.

7. Bake the galettes for 35 to 40 minutes, until the crust is golden brown. Let cool on a wire cooling rack. Heat the apricot fruit spread in the microwave or in a small saucepan over medium heat, then brush the tops and around the crusts of the galettes. Serve warm or at room temperature.

8. The galettes are best served the day they are made but will last well, tightly wrapped, at room temperature for up to 2 days.

Peanut Butter Ripple Ice Cream Pie

I am crazy about this crispy-rice crust. Even though the filling
is vegan ice cream, dairy lovers devour it, too.

SERVES 8

Nonstick vegetable oil cooking spray

Crust

1¼ cups (213 g) dark chocolate chips
  (vegan, if desired)

1 tablespoon smooth peanut butter

1 teaspoon coconut oil

Small pinch of kosher salt

4 cups (107 g) unsweetened crispy rice
  cereal

Ice Cream

2 cups (240 g) raw cashews

½ cup (120 ml) coconut milk, well shaken
  or whisked

6 tablespoons (90 ml) pure maple syrup

1½ teaspoons pure vanilla extract

Peanut Butter Ripple

½ cup (128 g) smooth peanut butter

¼ cup (60 ml) date syrup

1 tablespoon coconut milk, well shaken or
  whisked

⅛ teaspoon kosher salt

1. Spray a 9-inch springform pan with cooking spray.

2. For the crust: In a small microwave-safe glass bowl, melt the chocolate chips in 10-second intervals, stirring each time, until melted and smooth, being careful not to overheat the chocolate. Or melt in a heat-proof glass bowl set over a pan of simmering water (don't let the bowl touch the water). Add the peanut butter, coconut oil, and salt and whisk until smooth.

3. Put the rice cereal in a large bowl and add the chocolate mixture. Stir until the cereal is evenly coated. Scrape the mixture into the prepared pan and, using the back of a metal spoon, press an even layer over the bottom and about 1½ inches up the sides, making sure to press into the corners. Freeze for 20 minutes, or until set.

4. For the ice cream: Put the cashews in a small saucepan and cover with cold water by 2 inches. Place over medium-high heat and let come to a boil. Reduce the heat to medium and simmer for 10 minutes. Drain the cashews into a strainer and pass under cold water to cool. Shake out excess water.

5. Make the peanut butter ripple: In a small mixing bowl, stir together the peanut butter, date syrup, coconut milk, and salt until thick and creamy.

6. Back to the ice cream: In a blender or food processor, finely chop the cashews. Add the coconut milk, maple syrup, and vanilla. Puree for about 2 minutes, scraping down the sides as necessary, until very smooth. It will have the texture of hummus. Scrape into a large mixing bowl.

7. Spoon half of the ripple mixture into the ice cream base. Using a large spoon, gently fold in the ripple mixture to make a swirl pattern. Repeat with the remaining ripple mixture, being careful not to over stir so you don't lose the swirl. Spoon into the prepared crust. Use the tip of the spoon to make swooping patterns as you spread the ice cream over the crust.

8. Freeze for about 2 hours, until sliceable. If you freeze it longer, the pie will become very firm and impossible to slice; just let it warm up on the counter (this could take up to 30 minutes). Slice and serve.

Little Cherry Mousse Pies

Our vegan friends will especially enjoy these, but of course
they are for everyone. Cashews make a wholesome base, sweetened
only with black cherry fruit spread. The graham cracker "cups"
also add some sweetness to this delightful treat.

SERVES 8

Nonstick vegetable oil cooking spray

Crust

13 graham crackers

6 tablespoons (84 g) coconut oil, melted

Mousse

½ cup (60 g) raw cashews

¼ cup (60 ml) coconut milk, well shaken
  or whisked

½ cup (160 g) black cherry fruit spread

½ teaspoon pure vanilla extract

¼ cup (60 ml) aquafaba

Fresh berries, for serving

1. Position an oven rack in the middle of the oven. Preheat the oven to
350°F. Spray 8 cups of a 12-cup muffin pan with cooking spray.

2. For the crust: In a food processor, grind the graham crackers into fine
crumbs. Measure 1¾ cups (175 g) and put them in a small mixing bowl. Add
the coconut oil and stir well to combine. The crumbs should hold together
when pressed against the side of the bowl.

3. Divide the crumbs among the 8 prepared muffin cups and firmly press
them over the bottoms and up the sides. Bake for 8 to 10 minutes, until set.
Place the pan on a wire cooling rack and let cool completely.

4. For the mousse: Put the cashews in a small saucepan and cover with
cold water by 2 inches. Place over medium-high heat and let come to a
boil. Reduce the heat to medium and simmer for 10 minutes. Drain the
cashews into a strainer and pass under cold water to cool. Shake out
excess water.

5. In a blender or food processor, finely chop the cashews. Add the
coconut milk and puree for about 2 minutes, or until the mixture is smooth
and creamy, scraping down the sides with a silicone spatula as necessary.
Mix in the fruit spread and vanilla until well combined. Scrape the mixture
into a medium mixing bowl.

6. Add the aquafaba to the bowl of a stand mixer fitted with the whisk
attachment, or to a large mixing bowl with a hand mixer. Beat the aquafaba
on medium-high speed for 5 to 8 minutes, until stiff peaks form.

7. Fold half of the aquafaba into the cherry mixture, then gently fold in the
remaining aquafaba. Divide the mousse among the graham cracker crusts.
Refrigerate for at least 4 hours, or until chilled and set.

8. Using the tip of a paring knife, slide it between each crust and muffin cup
to pop out the pies. Serve the pies topped with fresh berries.

9. Keep stored in an airtight container in the refrigerator for up to 3 days.

Roasted Grape Turnovers

I keep phyllo dough in my freezer at all times so I can make
an emergency dessert like this one. These always impress; the roasted
grapes sweeten and a drizzle of honey tops it off.

MAKES 8

Eight 9 × 13-inch sheets frozen phyllo
dough, thawed in its packaging

6 tablespoons (3 ounces; 84 g) unsalted
butter, melted

½ cup (114 g) fresh ricotta cheese

½ recipe Roasted Grapes (page 152)

½ teaspoon anise seeds

2 teaspoons sesame seeds

Honey, for drizzling (optional)

1. Position an oven rack in the middle of the oven. Preheat the oven to 375°F. Line a large rimmed sheet pan with parchment paper.

2. To keep the phyllo sheets from drying out, place them on one half of a large dishcloth, lay a piece of plastic wrap over the top to cover, then cover with the other half of the cloth.

3. To form each turnover, place 1 sheet of phyllo on a clean work surface, with the short side closest to you.

4. Evenly brush half of the phyllo sheet lengthwise with some of the melted butter. Fold the sheet in half lengthwise to make a long strip. Lightly brush the entire top surface with butter.

5. Spoon a 1-tablespoon dollop of the ricotta on the bottom of the strip closest to you, about 1 inch above the edge. Top with 8 of the Roasted Grapes and sprinkle with a pinch of the anise seeds. (Be careful not to overstuff or they will burst as they bake.) Lift the bottom right corner over the filling to form a triangle and gently seal the edge. Continue folding up and over to maintain the triangle shape (like you would a flag) until you reach the end of the strip. Brush the top with butter and place on the prepared pan. Repeat with the remaining ingredients. Sprinkle the tops with the sesame seeds.

6. Bake the turnovers for 22 to 26 minutes, until golden brown and crisp.

7. Serve them hot, drizzled with a little honey (if using).

8. These are best served the day they are made.

Chocolate Profiteroles

This recipe revolutionized my favorite dessert.
We made the profiteroles gluten-free, and the chocolate sauce
is sweetened with our cherry compote.

MAKES 18

Cream Puffs

3/4 cup (180 ml) water

6 tablespoons (3 ounces; 84 g) unsalted
butter, cut into pieces

1/4 teaspoon kosher salt

3/4 cup (111 g) gluten-free baking flour,
spooned and leveled

3 large eggs, at cool room temperature

Chocolate Sauce

1 1/2 cups (360 ml) Cherry Compote (page
235)

2/3 cup (56 g) unsweetened cocoa
powder

6 tablespoons (90 ml) maple syrup

2 teaspoons pure vanilla extract

1/4 teaspoon kosher salt

1 1/2 cups (360 ml) heavy whipping cream

1. Position two oven racks toward the middle of the oven. Preheat the oven to 425°F. Line two large rimmed sheet pans with parchment paper.

2. For the cream puffs: In a medium saucepan, combine the water, butter, and salt over medium heat. Once the butter has melted and the mixture starts to boil, remove from the heat, add the flour all at once, and use a wooden spoon to stir it in. Return the pan to the heat and stir vigorously until the mixture comes together into a sticky ball. Continue to stir for 1 to 2 minutes more to dry out the mixture further (there will be a film at the bottom of the pan). Remove from the heat and let cool for 3 minutes, stirring occasionally to help it cool.

3. Add the eggs one at a time, stirring vigorously and making sure each egg is fully incorporated before adding the next. (The mixture will separate with each addition but come together quickly into a thick paste.) At the end, the paste should be smooth and hold its shape on the spoon.

4. Using two soup spoons, form 9 tall mounds of paste, each 1 1/2 inches in diameter and about 1 inch high, on each prepared pan, spacing them evenly; you should have a total of 18 mounds. Bake for 15 minutes, then reduce the heat to 375°F and bake for 20 to 25 minutes more, until golden brown and crisp. Do not open the oven door until the end of the baking, to check for doneness.

5. Remove the pans from the oven and turn the oven off. Poke a skewer into the side of each puff to release the steam. Return the pans to the oven, prop open the oven door, and let the puffs dry out as the oven cools. Then transfer the puffs to a wire cooling rack to cool completely.

6. For the chocolate sauce: In a blender, combine the Cherry Compote, cocoa powder, maple syrup, vanilla, and salt. Blend until very smooth. If it's a little thick, add 1 to 2 tablespoons water for desired consistency.

7. In the bowl of a stand mixer fitted with the whisk attachment, or in a large mixing bowl with a hand mixer, beat the cream on medium speed until soft peaks form. Add 3/4 cup of the chocolate sauce and beat until stiff peaks form.

8. To serve: Cut the puffs in half horizontally and remove the tops. Spoon the chocolate whipped cream onto the bottoms, then replace the tops. Warm the remaining chocolate sauce and drizzle over the profiteroles.

WE ALWAYS GO BACK HOME

When I was growing up, my mom was not a big dessert maker. Nor was she a dessert giver. She worked full-time as a social worker and commuted a long way, leaving little time for dessert preparation. She insisted on us eating a home-cooked dinner, which I often helped her with. This got me in the kitchen at a young age. But baking was never quite her "thing," nor was keeping sweet treats in the house regularly. This didn't stop me from always asking her "What's for dessert?" The answer would almost always be "Have a piece of fruit." It annoyed me every time. I, like most kids, didn't view fruit as a desirable dessert option. We had visions of luscious cakes, freshly baked cookies, or warm, fudgy brownies. To work around my mother's healthy habits, I learned how to bake independently, as I mention on page 190.

Occasionally, my mother or my grandmother would surprise my two sisters and me by making boxed chocolate pudding or brownies. The norm, however, was to be offered an orange, grapes, or grapefruit for dessert. Most often, I would turn it down. My mother or grandmother would try to market an apple as a "fancy apple," and they would cut it in a special jigsaw way. This did not "cut it" as I got older, but as a five-year-old, I will admit I was in awe of how the jagged edges of the "fancy" apple fit together.

When my kids were younger, they inevitably asked, "What's for dessert?" Since I do bake often, leftover treats are always around the kitchen. We all know kids never want what's easy, so when they were not satisfied with the available offerings, I could hear my mother's voice in my head as I continued the family tradition and offered them a piece of fruit.

Many of the recipes in this book are a nod to the good old days when fruit was The Treat in my house. The grated frozen grapes on page 155 are a perfect example. They could not be sweeter. We are armed with more nutritional information these days, so we know there is enough sugar in grapes that we don't need to add anything more for them to be satisfying, sweet enough, and not overindulgent.

"Many of the recipes in this book are a nod to the good old days when fruit was The Treat in my house."

The simple and basic Roasted Strawberries (page 225), Roasted Blueberries (page 234), and Roasted Grapes (page 152) are some of my favorites. The Honeydew Melon with Spicy Sesame Brittle (page 143), Slow-Roasted Orange Slices with Goat Cheese (page 151), and Papaya Granita (page 148) are just as delicious and simple to prepare, with a little something "fancy" added.

It's funny when we return to what our parents tried to teach us. I am clearly following in my mother's footsteps in writing a book that basically offers people fruit for dessert. I think the recipes on these pages are a little more appealing than an orange, but there is also nothing wrong with an apple for dessert, fancy or not.

Fruit

Macerated Berries with Strawberry Cream

When we shot the photos for this book, our fantastic crew got to taste everything. This simple recipe was demolished on the spot. Was it the cream, the coconut chips, or the berries? You decide.

SERVES 4

1 pound (454 g) fresh strawberries, hulled

One 6-ounce package (1½ cups; 170 g) fresh raspberries

1 tablespoon coconut sugar

1¼ cups (300 ml) heavy whipping cream

⅓ cup (107 g) strawberry fruit spread, plus more for serving

Unsweetened toasted coconut flakes, for serving

Finely grated fresh nutmeg, for serving

1. Slice the strawberries and put them in a medium mixing bowl. Add the raspberries and the coconut sugar and toss gently. Let stand for 10 to 15 minutes, stirring occasionally, until the juices start to run.

2. In the bowl of a stand mixer fitted with the whisk attachment, or in a large mixing bowl with a hand mixer, beat together the cream and the fruit spread on medium-high speed until soft peaks form.

3. Dividing evenly, spoon some of the berries into the bottom of four small glasses. Add a layer of the whipped cream, another spoonful of berries, and a final layer of whipped cream. Top with a small dollop of fruit spread, the coconut flakes, and a sprinkle of nutmeg.

Honeydew Melon with Spicy Sesame Brittle

This is a fun last-minute dessert. The brittle takes no time to
make, and you may already have most of these ingredients in your pantry.
I love the sweetness of the melon with the spicy brittle.

SERVES 4 TO 6

2 tablespoons sesame seeds

2 tablespoons coconut sugar

1 tablespoon hot (or regular) honey

¼ teaspoon extra virgin olive oil

⅛ teaspoon kosher salt

Honeydew melon, for serving

Cayenne pepper or ground chipotle, for
serving

1. Position an oven rack in the middle of the oven. Preheat the oven to
325°F. Line a large rimmed sheet pan with parchment paper.

2. Put the sesame seeds in a small skillet and place over medium heat. Toast
the sesame seeds, shaking the skillet often, for 3 to 5 minutes, until light
golden brown.

3. In a small mixing bowl, stir together the coconut sugar, honey, olive oil,
and salt. Add the sesame seeds and stir until well combined. The mixture
will be crumbly.

4. Evenly crumble the mixture over the prepared pan in an area that covers
about 6 × 6 inches.

5. Bake for 12 to 16 minutes, until amber in color. (It will spread out and
bubble a lot at first, then become one large piece.) Let the brittle cool
completely on the pan, then peel it off. It should be nice and crisp. If it's still
a little chewy, put it back in the oven for a few more minutes.

6. Scoop out bite-size pieces of the honeydew and divide among bowls.
Sprinkle with a little cayenne. Break the brittle into shards and serve with
the honeydew.

Grilled Cardamom-Honey Plums with Coconut Cream

I'd wait until summer to make this, when you will find better plums. The coconut cream is luscious, especially with the lime zest and honey.

SERVES 4

2 tablespoons honey

¼ teaspoon ground cardamom

½ teaspoon crushed red pepper (optional)

1 lime

4 ripe but firm plums, or other stone fruit, such as nectarines or peaches

One 5.4-ounce can coconut cream, cold

1. In a small bowl, combine the honey, cardamom, and crushed red pepper.

2. Finely grate the zest of the lime and set it aside. Juice half of the lime and measure 1 teaspoon. Stir the juice into the cardamom honey.

3. Heat the grill to medium-high.

4. Cut the plums in half and remove the stones. Place the plum halves cut side up on the grill. Brush with some of the cardamom honey and flip them over. Grill for 1 to 3 minutes, until the honey caramelizes and grill marks form. Flip and repeat once more, finishing with a final baste of the cardamom honey.

5. In the bowl of a stand mixer fitted with the whisk attachment, or in a large mixing bowl with a hand mixer, beat the coconut cream until thickened.

6. To serve, spoon the coconut cream into bowls and top with the plums. Sprinkle with a little lime zest and drizzle with any leftover cardamom honey.

Spiced Fig Compote

Perfect for a cozy winter eve. The flavors and fruits make
me want to stay home and eat this in front of a fire.

SERVES 4

12 dried white Turkish figs, stems removed

4 Medjool dates, pitted and halved

3 tablespoons honey

1 cinnamon stick

1 star anise

1 navel orange

For Serving (optional)

1 cup (240 ml) heavy whipping cream

3 tablespoons brandy (optional)

1 tablespoon pure maple syrup

1. Put the figs and dates in a small saucepan and cover with cold water by ½ inch. Add the honey, cinnamon stick, and star anise. Using a vegetable peeler, peel 4 long strips of zest from the orange and add to the pan, then juice the orange and add the juice.

2. Place the pan over medium-high heat and let come to a boil. Reduce the heat so it simmers gently for about 45 minutes, or until the figs are tender but still hold their shape and the liquid has cooked down and thickened. Stir occasionally as it simmers.

3. Remove the pan from the heat and let the compote cool to room temperature.

4. For serving: In the bowl of a stand mixer fitted with the whisk attachment, or in a large mixing bowl with a hand mixer, beat together the cream, brandy (if using), and the maple syrup until soft peaks form.

5. Divide the compote among shallow bowls and serve with a dollop of whipped cream (if using).

Papaya Granita

I'm crazy about papaya, especially with a hint of lime. This crowd-pleaser is hard to beat in summer.

SERVES 6

3 pounds (1.3 kg) ripe papaya, peeled, seeded, and cut into chunks (about 7 cups)

½ cup (120 ml) honey

Finely grated lime zest from 2 limes, for serving

¼ cup (60 ml) fresh lime juice (from 2 to 3 limes)

1. Put the papaya in a blender and add the honey. Blend until very smooth.

2. Grate the lime zest before juicing the limes. Wrap the zest tightly in plastic wrap and refrigerate until you're ready to serve the granita.

3. Add the lime juice to the blender. Blend to incorporate. Pour the mixture into an 8 × 8-inch square metal baking pan. Place the pan in the freezer and freeze for 3 to 4 hours, until completely frozen.

4. Right before serving, put 6 small glasses in the freezer to chill.

5. Use the tines of a fork to scrape the granita into fine shavings. Spoon into the glasses and top with the grated lime zest.

Slow-Roasted Orange Slices with Goat Cheese

Simple and beautiful, a dessert for our cheese-loving friends.

SERVES 4 TO 6

2 to 3 oranges, such as navel, Cara Cara, or blood (or a mix of all three)

8 ounces (227 g) fresh goat cheese

1. Position an oven rack in the middle of the oven. Preheat the oven to 200°F. Line a large rimmed sheet pan with parchment paper.

2. Slice the oranges into rounds as thinly as you can and no more than 1/8 inch thick. Remove any seeds.

3. Arrange the slices on the prepared pan in a single layer, spacing them close together but without touching.

4. Bake for 3 to 3½ hours, or until dried out and crisp but not brown. Some slices will crisp up faster than others, depending on thickness, so pull those from the oven while the others continue to bake. At the end of baking, turn the oven off and leave the slices in the oven to let them continue to dry out.

5. Take the goat cheese out of the refrigerator 30 minutes before you plan on serving to let it come to room temperature. Serve the orange slices alongside the goat cheese.

Roasted Grapes

Grapes, roasted to perfection, are the ultimate.
Their natural sweetness is condensed, so adding sugar is
unnecessary. They are perfect on their own, over ice cream,
or in our Roasted Grape Turnovers on page 133.

MAKES ABOUT 1¼ CUPS

1 to 2 bunches red seedless grapes (about
1½ pounds; 680 g)

Extra virgin olive oil

1. Position an oven rack in the middle of the oven. Preheat the oven to 375°F. Line a sheet pan with parchment paper.

2. Rinse the grapes and pat them dry. Remove the grapes from their stems and put them on the prepared pan. Drizzle them with a little olive oil and, using your hands, toss together, making sure each grape is lightly coated with oil.

3. Roast for 1 to 1½ hours, until the grapes start to shrivel and release their juices. They should be juicy and a little chewy at the same time. Place the pan on a wire cooling rack and let cool.

Green Grape Ice

I love to snack on frozen grapes, so I always have them in my freezer. I took it a step further and made them into ice. This is one of the easiest preparations in the book, though I am sorry about the noise from the food processor.

SERVES 4

3 cups (454 g) seedless green grapes

Finely grated grapefruit zest from
  1 grapefruit

Finely grated lime zest and juice from
  1 lime

1. Put the grapes in a zip-top plastic bag, spread them into a single layer, and freeze.

2. Right before serving, put 4 small glasses in the freezer to chill.

3. Put the frozen grapes in a food processor. Pulse several times until finely ground and fluffy.

4. Spoon the Green Grape Ice into the chilled glasses. Top with some grapefruit zest and lime zest, and a squeeze of lime.

Blue Cheese, Honeycomb, and Pears

You can find honeycomb online or at your favorite market.
I think this is such an elegant way to end a meal.

SERVES 4

8 ounces (227 g) blue cheese

4 ounces (113 g) honeycomb

2 pears, such as Bosc or Bartlett

1. Take the blue cheese out of the refrigerator 1 hour before you plan on serving to let it come to room temperature.

2. Divide the blue cheese and honeycomb among plates. Cut the pears in half lengthwise and, using a melon baller or small spoon, scoop out the cores. Slice the pears and serve them alongside the blue cheese and honeycomb.

Slow-Roasted-Peach Ice Cream

Well, it's not actually ice cream. This dairy-free dessert is all fruit,
nothing else. Using frozen peaches makes it a breeze.

SERVES 4

3 pounds (1.4 kg) frozen sliced peaches,
thawed

1. Position two oven racks toward the middle of the oven. Preheat the oven to 300°F. Line two large rimmed sheet pans with parchment paper.

2. Spread the peach slices over the pans in a single layer. Roast for 1½ to 2 hours, stirring halfway through, until the slices have released their juices and shrunk in size. They will feel a little leathery but should still be soft, not dried out. A little color around the edges is okay, but you don't want them brown.

3. Place the pans on wire cooling racks and let the peaches cool completely. Transfer the peaches to 2 large zip-top plastic bags and spread them into single layers so the peach slices freeze individually. Freeze.

4. Put the frozen peaches in a food processor. Let them sit for 2 to 3 minutes to thaw a little. Then turn on the processor and let it run for 3 to 5 minutes, scraping down the sides as necessary with a silicone spatula, until the peaches become smooth and creamy.

5. Spoon the ice cream into small bowls and serve. You can also store it in the freezer for up to 1 week, until you are ready to serve.

Caramelized Pears with Cider and Hazelnuts

These are a cozy fall treat, sweetened with only apple cider and raisins.

SERVES 4

4 firm but ripe pears, such as Bosc

2 tablespoons cold unsalted butter or vegan butter

1 cup (240 ml) apple cider

¼ cup (40 g) golden raisins

⅛ teaspoon finely grated nutmeg

Tiny pinch of kosher salt

¼ cup (36 g) roasted whole hazelnuts, skins removed, chopped

1. Position an oven rack in the middle of the oven. Preheat the oven to 400°F.

2. Peel the pears and cut them in half lengthwise. Use a melon baller or small spoon to scoop out the cores.

3. Place a large ovenproof skillet over medium-high heat. Once it's hot, add 1 tablespoon of the butter and swirl the skillet to coat the bottom. Place the pears cut sides down in the skillet. Cook for 3 to 4 minutes, until the undersides are golden brown. Transfer the skillet to the oven and bake for 10 to 15 minutes, until the pears are tender and can be easily pierced with the tip of a paring knife.

4. Transfer the pears to a large serving dish or bowls, cut sides up.

5. Add the apple cider, raisins, and nutmeg to the skillet and return it to medium-high heat. Let simmer rapidly for 4 to 6 minutes, until the apple cider reduces to about ¼ cup (the bubbles will get bigger as it reduces). Add the remaining 1 tablespoon butter and the salt and swirl the skillet until the butter melts. Remove from the heat.

6. Pour the glaze over the pears and sprinkle with the hazelnuts.

Dutch Baby with Apple Cider Syrup

I've been making this for my entire adult life. It's a low-sugar breakfast that we think makes the perfect dessert. Ours is sweetened by reducing apple cider into a syrup, then drizzling it on top.

SERVES 4 TO 6

4 large eggs

½ cup (74 g) gluten-free baking flour, spooned and leveled

½ cup (120 ml) whole milk

1 teaspoon pure vanilla extract

¼ teaspoon kosher salt

⅛ teaspoon finely grated nutmeg

4 tablespoons (2 ounces; 57 g) unsalted butter

1 cup (240 ml) apple cider

¼ cup (60 g) crème fraîche, for serving

Fresh berries, for serving

1 lemon, for serving

1. Position an oven rack in the middle of the oven. Preheat the oven to 425°F. Place a 10-inch ovenproof skillet with straight sides (preferably cast iron) in the oven while it heats up.

2. In a medium bowl, whisk together the eggs. Add the flour and whisk until smooth, then whisk in the milk, vanilla, salt, and nutmeg. (Alternatively, you can blend everything together in a blender.)

3. Once the skillet is nice and hot, add the butter. Put the skillet back in the oven for about 1 minute to let the butter brown (be careful it doesn't burn). Carefully pour 2 tablespoons of the melted butter into the batter and whisk it in, leaving the remaining 2 tablespoons butter in the skillet.

4. Immediately pour the batter into the hot skillet, then slide it back into the oven. Bake for 15 to 18 minutes, until golden brown and puffed.

5. While the Dutch Baby bakes, pour the apple cider into a small saucepan. Place over medium-high heat and let the apple cider come to a boil. Continue to boil for 6 to 8 minutes, until the apple cider cooks down to about 2 tablespoons and starts to thicken. Remove from the heat and cool for about 1 minute; it should thicken to a syrup. If it's a little too thin, just boil for another minute.

6. Drizzle the crème fraîche over the hot Dutch Baby, then scatter in the berries. Next, pour on the hot apple cider syrup and squeeze a little fresh lemon juice over the top. Slice and serve immediately.

Frozen Yogurt with Cherry Compote and Chickpea Brittle

A few elements come together to make a unique—
and somewhat healthful, dare I say?—dessert.

SERVES 4

Frozen Yogurt

32 ounces (907 g) unsweetened
  Greek yogurt or plant-based yogurt
  (about 3¾ cups)

Brittle

One 15-ounce can chickpeas, drained,
  rinsed, and patted dry (reserve
  aquafaba for Chocolate Meringue
  Kisses, page 56)

1 tablespoon extra virgin olive oil

½ cup (43 g) sliced almonds

2 teaspoons sesame seeds

3 tablespoons honey

¼ teaspoon ground cinnamon

Small pinch of kosher salt

1 recipe Cherry Compote (page 235)

1. For the frozen yogurt: Spoon the yogurt into ice trays and freeze for about 2 hours, or until completely frozen.

2. For the brittle: Position an oven rack in the middle of the oven. Preheat the oven to 400°F. Line a large rimmed sheet pan with parchment paper.

3. Coarsely chop the chickpeas and put them on the prepared pan. Drizzle with the olive oil and, using your hands, roll them around so they are evenly coated. Bake for 20 minutes to dry out the chickpeas.

4. Push the chickpeas toward the center of the pan and add the almonds and sesame seeds. Drizzle with the honey and stir well to coat. Spread the mixture out across the pan so it crisps up evenly. Bake for 10 to 12 minutes, until the almonds are golden brown. Place the pan on a wire cooling rack and sprinkle with the cinnamon and salt. The brittle will crisp up as it cools.

5. Put the frozen yogurt cubes in a food processor. Let them sit for 5 to 10 minutes to thaw a little, then let the processor run until the yogurt is smooth and creamy, stirring as necessary.

6. Divide the yogurt among bowls and top with Cherry Compote and brittle.

Crustless Apple Crumble Pie

No crust, just a little crumb topping keeps this dessert well within the range of "moderation." It can be made dairy-free as well.

SERVES 8

Nonstick vegetable oil cooking spray

Crumble

½ cup (54 g) super-fine almond flour, spooned and leveled

¼ cup (37 g) gluten-free baking flour, spooned and leveled

⅓ cup (65 g) coconut sugar

½ teaspoon kosher salt

4 tablespoons (2 ounces; 57 g) cold unsalted butter or vegan butter, cut into small pieces

½ cup (64 g) walnuts, coarsely chopped

Apples

3½ pounds (1.6 kg; 6 or 7) apples, such as Honey Crisp

3 tablespoons coconut sugar

1 tablespoon honey

½ teaspoon ground cinnamon

Vanilla ice cream, for serving (optional)

1. Position an oven rack in the middle of the oven. Preheat the oven to 375°F. Spray a 9-inch springform pan with cooking spray (this will help the parchment paper stick to the pan). Line the bottom and up the sides of the pan with a large piece of parchment paper, leaving a 2-inch overhang all the way around the rim of the pan (you may need to use 2 pieces of parchment, depending on the width of your roll).

2. For the crumble: In a medium mixing bowl, stir together the almond flour, baking flour, coconut sugar, and salt. Add the butter and, using your fingertips or a pastry cutter, work the butter into the dry mixture until large moist crumbs form. Mix in the walnuts. Refrigerate while you slice the apples.

3. For the apples: Peel and core the apples. Thinly slice the apples to about ⅛ inch thick (a mandoline slicer really helps) and put them in a large bowl. Add the coconut sugar, honey, and cinnamon and, using your hands, gently toss to coat the apples.

4. In the prepared pan, add one quarter of the apples at a time in an even layer, making sure the apple slices are compact before you add the next round of apples. The apples should just about reach the top of the pan.

5. Scatter the crumble topping over the apples. Place the springform pan on a large rimmed sheet pan to catch any juices that may escape and slide into the oven. Bake for 55 to 70 minutes, until the apples are bubbling and tender when you insert the tip of a paring knife into them. Tent a piece of foil over the top if the crumble starts to brown too much.

6. Place both pans on a wire cooling rack and let the pie cool completely. When ready to serve, remove the ring. Slide the pie onto a serving plate or a cutting board.

7. Slice the pie and serve with vanilla ice cream (if using).

8. The pie is best served the day it's made.

Ours vs. Theirs

We thought it would be interesting to compare how much sugar there is in our recipes vs. more traditional ones. We've also noted the less-processed sugars we use, making our recipes sweet . . . but not too sweet.

Our Chocolate Layer Cake

Cake: 1 cup maple syrup
Frosting: 5 tablespoons maple syrup

TOTAL SUGAR
1 cup plus 5 tablespoons maple syrup

Typical Chocolate Layer Cake

Cake: 2 cups granulated sugar
Frosting: 3 cups confectioners' sugar

TOTAL SUGAR
5 cups sugar

Our Lemon Bundt Cake

Cake: ¾ cup maple syrup plus
½ cup coconut sugar
icing: ¼ cup maple syrup

TOTAL SUGAR
1½ cups

Typical Bundt Cakes

Cake: 2 cups granulated sugar
icing: 2 cups confectioners' sugar

TOTAL SUGAR
4 cups

Our Chocolate Chip Cookies

½ cup coconut sugar plus
¼ cup maple syrup

TOTAL SUGAR
¾ cup

Toll House Chocolate Chip Cookies

¾ cup granulated sugar plus
¾ cup brown sugar

TOTAL SUGAR
1½ cups

Our Butter Pecan Ice Cream

TOTAL SUGAR
¼ cup honey

Typical Ice Cream

TOTAL SUGAR
1 cup granulated sugar

Our Chocolate Brownies

Sweetened only with dates, sweet potato, and dark chocolate chips

Typical Chocolate Brownies

TOTAL SUGAR
1 to 2 cups granulated sugar

Our Lemon Bars

TOTAL SUGAR
½ cup plus 2 tablespoons maple syrup

Typical Lemon Bars

TOTAL SUGAR
1½ cups granulated sugar

Our Oat Milk Caramel

TOTAL SUGAR
¼ cup honey

Typical Caramel Sauce

TOTAL SUGAR
½ cup granulated sugar

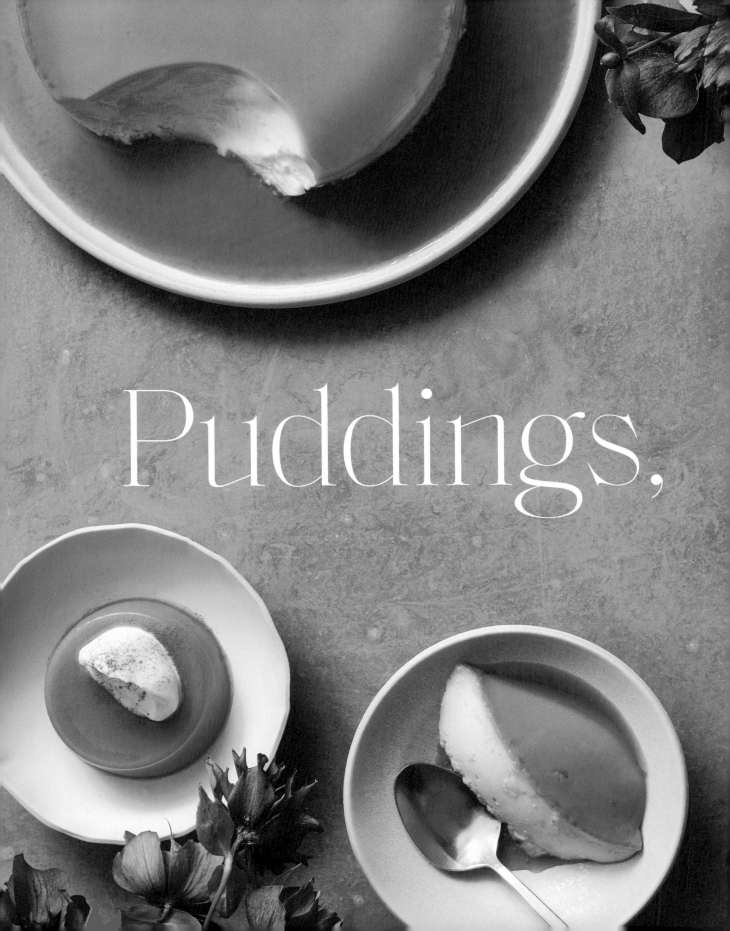

Puddings,

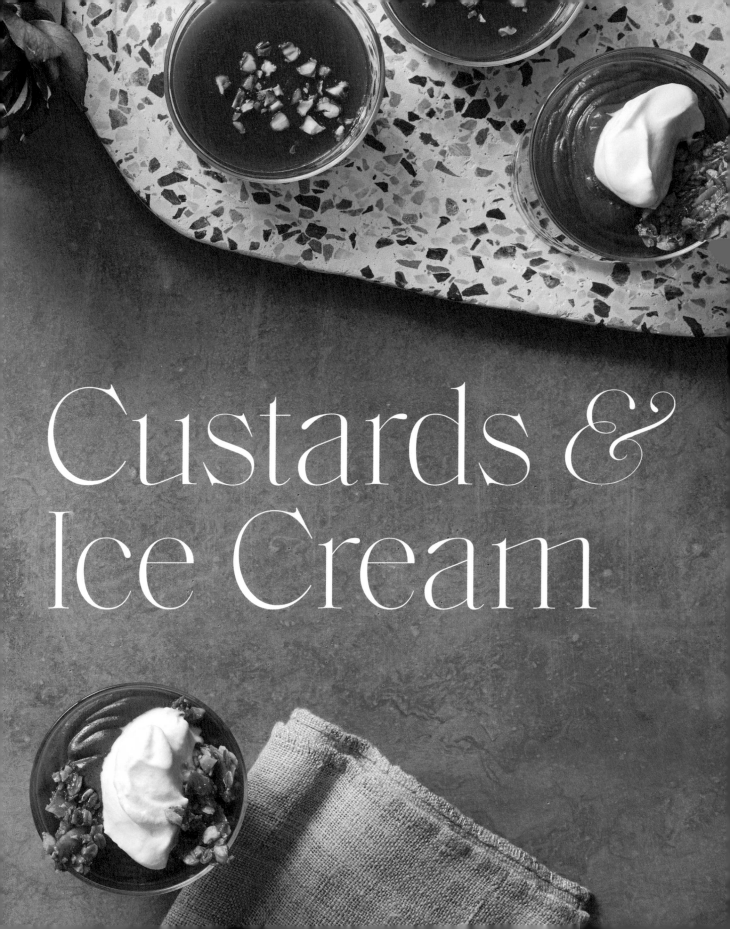

Custards & Ice Cream

Flan

I love flan so much that we made sure we included it in this book. We felt we needed to keep it traditional, full of sugar, and as delicious as ever.

SERVES 6 TO 8

Caramel

3/4 cup (150 g) granulated sugar

2 tablespoons water

1/2 teaspoon fresh lemon juice

Custard

4 large eggs

2 large egg yolks

2/3 cup (133 g) granulated sugar

2 cups whole milk

1 cup (240 ml) heavy whipping cream

11/2 teaspoons pure vanilla extract

1/8 teaspoon kosher salt

1. Position an oven rack in the middle of the oven. Preheat the oven to 325°F.

2. For the caramel: In a medium skillet, stir together the sugar, water, and lemon juice. (I like a nonstick skillet for this because every drop of caramel will release when poured out, but it does make it difficult to see the color of the caramel. A regular skillet is fine, too.) Place over medium heat. As it heats up, the sugar will start to liquefy and bubble. Once it starts to turn golden brown around the edges, start swirling the skillet. It will then start to caramelize throughout. Keep swirling as it turns a deep amber and just starts to smoke. Immediately pour the caramel into an 8-inch soufflé dish or baking dish that is about 31/2 inches deep. Set aside. Whatever you do, don't touch the hot caramel.

3. For the custard: In a large bowl, whisk together the eggs, egg yolks, and sugar. While gently whisking, gradually pour in the milk, then the cream, vanilla, and salt. Pour the mixture into the prepared soufflé dish.

4. Fill a large baking dish or roasting pan with 1/2 inch of very hot tap water and place in the oven. Place the soufflé dish in the water. Add more hot water so it reaches about halfway up the sides of the soufflé dish.

5. Bake for 45 to 55 minutes, until just set around the edges with quite a little wobble in the middle. (It will continue to set up as it cools.) Transfer to a wire cooling rack. After about 5 minutes, carefully lift the soufflé dish from the water bath and place on the cooling rack. Let cool to room temperature, then cover tightly, and refrigerate overnight and up to 3 days.

6. To unmold, slide a paring knife straight down between the edge of the custard and the dish. Run the knife around the custard to loosen, making sure not to cut into it. Place a large serving plate over the top of the dish and, holding them tightly together, quickly invert the two. The flan will slide onto the plate along with the caramel (give it a little tap, if it doesn't release). Lift off the soufflé dish. Serve right away.

Warm Lemon Pudding Cakes

These pudding cakes are light and airy, like a soufflé, but sweetened only with honey. They are a must! PS: They reheat beautifully with a zap in the microwave.

SERVES 8

4 large eggs

2/3 cup (160 ml) honey

1 tablespoon unsalted butter, melted

1/4 cup (37 g) gluten-free baking flour, spooned and leveled

1/4 teaspoon kosher salt

Finely grated lemon zest from 2 lemons

1/3 cup (80 ml) fresh lemon juice (from 1 to 2 lemons)

1¼ cups (300 ml) milk or plant-based milk, such as oat, almond, or cashew

Maple Whipped Cream (page 236), for serving (optional)

1. Position an oven rack in the middle of the oven. Preheat the oven to 350°F.

2. Separate the eggs and put the whites in the bowl of a stand mixer fitted with the whisk attachment, or in a large mixing bowl with a hand mixer. (Be sure that no trace of egg yolk gets into the egg whites.) Put the yolks in a large mixing bowl.

3. Add the honey to the egg yolks and whisk together. Then whisk in the melted butter, flour, and salt. Now whisk in the lemon zest, lemon juice, and milk.

4. Beat the egg whites on medium speed until creamy, medium peaks form.

5. Using a silicone spatula, gently stir the egg whites, one half at a time, into the lemon mixture.

6. Place eight high-sided 6-ounce ramekins on a large rimmed sheet pan. Ladle in the batter, filling the ramekins three-quarters full. (Alternatively, you can use an ungreased 8-inch soufflé dish.) Bake for 32 to 36 minutes, until the top is springy to the touch and golden brown.

7. Serve warm, topped with a dollop of the Maple Whipped Cream (if using).

No-Churn Butter Pecan Ice Cream

These days I'm either buying a pint of ice cream at the store or it's got to be no-churn. And while I'm at it, make it butter pecan.

SERVES 4 TO 6

3/4 cup (84 g) pecans

1 recipe Oat Milk Caramel (page 224)

1 cup (240 ml) heavy whipping cream

1. Position an oven rack in the middle of the oven. Preheat the oven to 350°F.

2. Spread the pecans on a small rimmed sheet pan. Bake for 8 to 10 minutes, until fragrant and crisp. When cool, finely chop them and measure 1/2 cup.

3. In a medium mixing bowl, stir together the pecans and the Oat Milk Caramel. Let cool completely.

4. In the bowl of a stand mixer fitted with the whisk attachment, or in a large mixing bowl with a hand mixer, beat the cream on medium-high speed until stiff peaks form.

5. Add half of the whipped cream to the caramel mixture and fold in until well combined. Then fold in the remaining whipped cream. Scrape into a freezer-proof container and freeze for about 2 hours, or until firm. Scoop and serve.

Coconut Milk Pudding with Plum Jelly

A pudding for our vegan friends. The flavor combination of coconut, plums, and pistachios makes this one worth the effort. You can make this a day ahead when you know you have vegans coming for lunch or dinner.

SERVES 4

Pudding

1¼ cups (300 ml) coconut milk, well shaken or whisked

1 cup (240 ml) water

3 tablespoons pure maple syrup

¼ teaspoon kosher salt

3 tablespoons plus 1 teaspoon cornstarch

1 teaspoon pure vanilla extract

Plum Jelly

8 ounces (227 g) ripe black plums (about 3 small)

2 tablespoons pure maple syrup

3 tablespoons water

1 teaspoon fresh lemon juice

Tiny pinch of kosher salt

¼ cup (30 g) roasted, salted pistachios, chopped, for serving

1. For the pudding: In a small saucepan, combine the coconut milk, ¾ cup of the water, the maple syrup, and the salt over medium-high heat. Stir occasionally as it comes to a boil.

2. In a small bowl, stir together the cornstarch and the remaining ¼ cup water. While whisking the coconut milk mixture, slowly add the cornstarch mixture. Continue to whisk as it comes back to a boil (it will start to thicken). Once the pudding is boiling, whisk rapidly for 1 minute more. Remove from the heat and whisk in the vanilla.

3. Divide the pudding among four small glasses or cups. Cover each glass with plastic wrap and refrigerate for at least 4 hours, or overnight, until chilled.

4. For the plum jelly: Cut the plums in half and remove the stones. Slice the plums into thin wedges and put them in a small saucepan. Add the maple syrup, water, lemon juice, and salt. Place over medium heat and let come to a simmer. Then reduce the heat to medium-low and simmer for 6 to 10 minutes, stirring often, until the plums break down completely and thicken. Using the back of a spoon, press the mixture through a strainer to remove the skins. Let the jelly cool for 10 minutes, then refrigerate until chilled.

5. To serve, spoon the jelly over the puddings, then top with the pistachios.

6. The puddings, wrapped tightly, can be refrigerated for up to 4 days, but it's best to top with the pistachios right before serving.

Rice Pudding
with Date Broiled Pineapple

Nothing is quite as satisfying as rice pudding.
We use a fraction of the sugar, and it comes in the form
of dried and fresh fruit, and a little date syrup.

SERVES 6

3 cups (720 ml) plant-based milk, such as oat, almond, or cashew

½ cup (120 ml) coconut milk, well shaken or whisked

½ cup (80 g) golden raisins

6 to 8 Medjool dates (132 to 176 g), pitted and sliced

1 cinnamon stick

⅛ teaspoon kosher salt

1 navel orange

½ cup (90 g) arborio rice

1 teaspoon pure vanilla extract

Two ½-inch-thick round slices of fresh, ripe pineapple, skin removed

Date syrup, for drizzling

1. In a medium saucepan, combine the milk, coconut milk, raisins, dates, cinnamon stick, and salt. Finely grate the zest of the orange directly into the saucepan.

2. Put the rice in a fine strainer and rinse under cold running water. Shake out excess water and add the rice to the saucepan.

3. Place the saucepan over medium-high heat and let come to a boil, stirring a few times. Reduce the heat to medium-low and simmer gently for about 20 minutes, or until the rice is tender and the mixture is creamy but not too thick (it will thicken more as it cools). Discard the cinnamon stick.

4. Stir in the vanilla.

5. Divide the pudding among six small glasses or cups.

6. Position an oven rack about 6 inches from the top. Heat the broiler to high. Line a large rimmed sheet pan with foil.

7. Slice the pineapple rounds into small bite-size triangles, avoiding the core.

8. Arrange the pineapple pieces in a single layer on the prepared pan. Drizzle with date syrup to lightly coat the tops. Broil for 3 to 5 minutes, until the date syrup starts to bubble and caramelize.

9. Serve the warm rice pudding topped with the pineapple.

Watermelon Pudding

This traditional Sicilian dessert usually contains copious amounts
of sugar. We went with a little honey instead.

SERVES 6

1 small seedless watermelon

¼ cup (28 g) cornstarch

3 tablespoons honey

1 teaspoon pure vanilla extract

Tiny pinch of kosher salt

½ recipe Maple Whipped Cream (page 236), for serving

Ground cinnamon, for serving

1. Scoop out large pieces of the watermelon to measure 6 cups and put into a blender. Puree until smooth, then pour through a fine-mesh strainer. This should yield 3 cups (710 ml) of juice.

2. In a small bowl, stir together the cornstarch and ¼ cup of the watermelon juice.

3. Pour the remaining juice into a small saucepan and place over medium-high heat. Whisk in the honey. Let come to a boil. While constantly whisking the boiling juice, slowly pour in the cornstarch mixture. Reduce the heat to medium and simmer for about 2 minutes, whisking rapidly, or until thickened enough to coat the back of a spoon. Remove from the heat and stir in the vanilla and salt.

4. Divide the pudding among six small glasses or cups. Cover each glass with plastic wrap. Refrigerate for at least 4 hours, or overnight, until completely chilled and set.

5. To unmold, run a paring knife around each pudding and let it slide onto a small bowl or serving plate. Or you can serve them in the glasses. Serve topped with a dollop of the Maple Whipped Cream and a sprinkle of cinnamon.

6. The puddings, wrapped tightly, can be refrigerated for up to 4 days, but it's best to top with the whipped cream right before serving.

Apricot Custard

Custard lovers, we've taken the sugar out and used dried apricots to sweeten. You'll never go back.

SERVES 6

4 large eggs

1 recipe (1 cup; 262 g) Apricot Puree (page 229)

2 cups (480 ml) half-and-half

1 teaspoon pure vanilla extract

⅛ teaspoon kosher salt

Finely grated nutmeg, for the top

1. Position an oven rack in the middle of the oven. Preheat the oven to 350°F.

2. In a large mixing bowl, whisk together the eggs. Add the Apricot Puree and whisk until well incorporated. Add the half-and-half, vanilla, and salt and whisk together.

3. Pour the custard into an 8-inch soufflé dish or baking dish that is about 3½ inches deep. Grate some nutmeg over the top.

4. Fill a large baking dish or roasting pan with ½ inch of very hot tap water and place in the oven. Place the soufflé dish in the water. Add more hot water so it reaches about halfway up the sides of the soufflé dish.

5. Bake for 40 to 45 minutes, until the custard is just set around the edges but with a little wobble in the middle. (It will continue to set up as it cools.) Transfer to a wire cooling rack. After about 5 minutes, carefully lift the soufflé dish from the water bath and place on the cooling rack to let cool. Serve the custard slightly warm or cover tightly with plastic wrap, refrigerate for about 3 hours or up to 3 days, and serve chilled.

Chocolate Peanut Butter Pudding with Oat Clusters

This is hugely popular in my house because of the sweet, creamy, and crunchy trifecta.

SERVES 6

10 Medjool dates (220 g), pitted

About 3 cups boiling water, for plumping the dates

¼ cup (21 g) unsweetened cocoa powder

3 tablespoons cornstarch

½ teaspoon kosher salt

2 cups (480 ml) plant-based milk, such as oat, almond, or cashew, or whole milk

3 tablespoons smooth peanut butter

1 teaspoon pure vanilla extract

Maple Whipped Cream (page 236), for serving (optional)

Oat Clusters (page 188), for serving

1. Put the dates in a small mixing bowl. Add the boiling water to cover them by 1 inch and let stand for 10 minutes, or until very soft. Use tongs to pluck the dates out of the water (save the water) and put them in a food processor. Add 3 to 4 tablespoons of the reserved date water (enough to make the dates puree easily). Puree the dates until completely smooth and creamy, scraping down the sides as necessary with a silicone spatula.

2. In a small saucepan, whisk together the cocoa powder, cornstarch, and salt. Whisk in ½ cup of the milk until smooth and without lumps (make sure to get into the corners). Whisk in the date puree, peanut butter, and another ½ cup milk. Then whisk in the remaining 1 cup milk.

3. Place the saucepan over medium heat. Whisk often as the pudding heats up. Once it starts to bubble and thicken, whisk constantly for 30 seconds more, making sure to get into the corners of the pan. Remove the pudding from the heat and whisk in the vanilla.

4. Divide the pudding evenly among six small glasses or cups. Wrap each glass tightly with plastic wrap. Refrigerate for at least 4 hours, or until chilled.

5. Serve the puddings topped with the Maple Whipped Cream (if using) and Oat Clusters.

Oat Clusters

2 tablespoons pure maple syrup

1 tablespoon coconut sugar

1 tablespoon water

1/8 teaspoon kosher salt

1 teaspoon coconut oil

1/2 teaspoon pure vanilla extract

1/4 cup (37 g) coarsely chopped roasted, salted peanuts

1/4 cup (15 g) unsweetened coconut flakes

1/4 cup (24 g) gluten-free old-fashioned rolled oats

1. Position an oven rack in the middle of the oven. Preheat the oven to 325°F. Line a large rimmed sheet pan with parchment paper.

2. In a small saucepan, combine the maple syrup, coconut sugar, water, and salt over medium heat. Let it come to a boil, swirling the pan occasionally as it does. Once the coconut sugar melts, remove the pan from the heat. Stir in the coconut oil and vanilla. Add the peanuts, coconut flakes, and oats and stir well to coat.

3. Scrape the oat mixture onto the prepared pan and press into a single layer (about 1/4 inch thick).

4. Bake for 25 to 30 minutes, until golden brown and crisp (it will crisp more as it cools). Once cool, break up into clusters.

THE BEAUTY OF BAKING

I've always been a baker. Since I was seven years old, I've loved to bake treats for my family and friends. As I mentioned earlier, devil's food cake was always my favorite to make, along with brownies and chocolate chip cookies. I learned to bake using ready-made mixes, and as I got older, I progressed to making recipes from scratch. As an adult, I am comforted by memories of being a young, independent girl, baking alone while my parents were at work. Surprising and delighting them with my creations was thrilling for me after they returned home from a long day.

Baking is both relaxing and exciting for me. I start by reading the recipe a few times, thinking it through, and creating a plan for the execution. Baking requires precise and accurate measurements, which is why many people dislike it intensely. For me, this level of precision gives me confidence that the recipe will turn out as expected. Restraint is required as you await the final product—for instance, stop yourself from opening the oven too early in anticipation, which would likely cause your cake or soufflé to deflate. Then, the exciting part comes, and you take the dessert out of the oven. But first you most likely have to let it cool. For baking, patience is one of the most important tools to have in your toolbox. Since I need to work on that in all areas of my life, why not build that muscle and produce a delicious result?

Baking is fun, and especially so when you are making an old favorite. I have a chocolate cake recipe in *Food Swings* that I love to make for my husband's, kids', and friends' birthdays. It comes out perfectly every time. I change the icing depending on the person. Jerry likes a peanut butter frosting, whereas Sascha loves strawberry. Julian and Shep both like chocolate. While it's second nature for me to make, it's still special for the birthday girl or boy to receive.

Over the years, as people's food issues have become more significant and prevalent, I've had to learn how to adjust to gluten-free and vegan needs. In *Vegan, at Times*, we perfected a strawberry pie, mint chip ice cream, and chocolate pudding that are dairy- and gluten-free. Throughout this book, you will find that approximately 90 percent of the recipes are gluten-free, many are vegan, and almost all are lower in sugar or contain no sugar at all.

Putting in the time and energy to make someone a mouthwatering treat is a splendid way to show your love. You are also building a skill you can use for the rest of your life. I like being someone who shows up to your house with homemade cookies and treats. That smile that greets you at the door is the greatest reward.

I appreciate being a baker in this complicated and busy world. The precision, the discipline, and the creative expression all calm and soothe my New York City nerves. When you've spent some time and energy crafting a birthday cake for a loved one, the moment it lands in front of them mid-song is gratifying. If your baking is like mine, your results might not be as polished as store-bought would be, but most would agree that a birthday cake made from scratch tastes better than a store-bought one. That's because it's made with the most exquisite secret ingredient: love.

A
Quick
Fix

Sweet Potato Caramel Corn

This recipe has less sugar than a similar one from my second book, *Double Delicious.* Just know you will likely end up overdosing on this, as Sara and I always do in our test kitchen.

MAKES 6 CUPS

1 small sweet potato, such as garnet yam

1 tablespoon extra virgin olive oil

½ cup (112 g) popcorn kernels

1 tablespoon coconut oil

⅓ cup (80 ml) honey

½ teaspoon ground cinnamon

Kosher salt, for sprinkling

1. Position two oven racks toward the middle of the oven. Preheat the oven to 400°F. Prick the sweet potato a few times with the tines of a fork. Place on a small rimmed sheet pan and bake for 35 to 45 minutes, until very tender. When cool enough to handle, scoop the flesh into a food processor and puree until very smooth. Measure ½ cup (120 g); save any remaining puree for another use.

2. Reduce the oven temperature to 350°F. Line two large rimmed sheet pans with parchment paper.

3. In a large pot, heat the olive oil over medium heat. Add the popcorn, cover tightly, and wait for it to start popping. Once it does, shake the pot often until the popping slows to a near stop. You should get about 10 cups of popcorn. Divide the popcorn evenly between the prepared pans.

4. In a small nonstick skillet, melt the coconut oil over medium heat. Add the sweet potato puree and honey and whisk together. Cook for 5 minutes, whisking often as it bubbles, until the moisture from the sweet potato cooks away (it will be thick). Remove from the heat and whisk in the cinnamon.

5. Dividing evenly between the two pans, scrape the mixture over the popcorn. Use two spoons to toss together to evenly distribute the sweet potato mixture. Spread the coated popcorn out into single layers.

6. Bake for about 15 minutes, or until the sweet potato caramel is set (it will become crisp as it cools). Immediately sprinkle with a little salt. Let cool completely, then serve.

7. The popcorn is best served the day it's made but can be stored in an airtight container for up to 3 days.

Raspberry Patties

Do not be deceived by how professional
these look. They could not be easier to prepare and they
are a huge "WOW" any time of day.

MAKES 12

1¼ cups (150 g) fresh or frozen
  raspberries

1 tablespoon pure maple syrup

2 tablespoons chia seeds

1¾ cups (298 g) dark chocolate chips
  (vegan, if desired)

1 teaspoon coconut oil

1. In a small saucepan, combine the raspberries and maple syrup over medium-high heat. Let come to a boil, then reduce the heat to medium so it simmers. Simmer for 3 to 5 minutes, until the raspberries break down. Remove from the heat and stir in the chia seeds. Let cool to room temperature, stirring every so often to make sure the chia seeds are well incorporated.

2. Evenly divide the raspberry filling among the cups of a 12-cup muffin pan (about 1 tablespoon for each cup). Spread the mixture to evenly cover the bottoms. Freeze for about 45 minutes, or until completely frozen.

3. Line a large rimmed sheet pan with parchment paper.

4. In a small microwave-safe glass bowl, combine the chocolate chips and coconut oil. Melt in 10-second intervals, stirring each time, until melted and smooth, being careful not to overheat the chocolate. Or melt in a heat-proof glass bowl set over a pan of simmering water (don't let the bowl touch the water).

5. Run the tip of a paring knife around the raspberry disks, then pop them out.

6. Using a fork, dip each disk into the chocolate to coat completely in a thin layer of chocolate, shaking off any extra. Use the edge of the bowl to scrape off the excess chocolate from the bottoms.

7. Since the raspberry disks are frozen, the chocolate will set immediately. The raspberry filling will thaw after about 5 minutes, then they will be ready to serve. Keep stored in the refrigerator for up to 1 week.

Caramels

Okay, these are not real caramels. But they are cute, brown, and, luckily, far healthier and easy to make. So, we call them caramels.

MAKES 12

6 Medjool dates (132 g), pitted

¼ cup (64 g) almond butter

¼ cup (24 g) gluten-free old-fashioned rolled oats

2 teaspoons finely grated peeled fresh ginger

⅛ teaspoon kosher salt

1. In a food processor, combine the dates, almond butter, oats, ginger, and salt. Pulse until almost completely smooth, with only some flecks of oats remaining.

2. Shape into 2-inch-long bars. Serve right away or keep stored in an airtight container in the refrigerator for up to 2 weeks.

Fruit Spring Rolls

Kids delight in these as much as adults do. It's fun
to get your family and friends to build their own. They're
refreshing, light, and lovely on a summer day.

MAKES 10

Spring Rolls

1 cup (170 g) fresh, ripe pineapple, peeled
and cut into 2-inch sticks

1 cup (152 g) watermelon, cut into 2-inch
sticks

1 apple, such as Honey Crisp, cut into
2-inch sticks

Finely grated zest of 1 lime

Finely grated zest of ½ navel orange

8 fresh mint leaves, chopped

Ten 9-inch spring roll rice paper wrappers

2 fresh kiwis, peeled and cut into thin
rounds

Dipping Sauce

1 cup (220g) full-fat or low-fat cottage
cheese

2 tablespoons honey, plus more for
drizzling

Ground cinnamon, for sprinkling

1. For the spring rolls: In a large mixing bowl, combine the pineapple, watermelon, apple, lime zest, orange zest, and mint. Gently toss to coat.

2. Fill a large bowl with very hot water. Dip a rice paper wrapper into the water until it just starts to soften (this should take 15 to 30 seconds). Shake off excess water. Lay the wrapper on a smooth work surface.

3. Place a small, tightly packed pile of the mixed fruit in the middle of the wrapper. Lay 2 kiwi rounds on top. Roll up like a tiny burrito: fold the ends over, then roll up tightly. Repeat with the remaining wrappers and fruit.

4. For the dipping sauce: In a blender, combine the cottage cheese and honey. Blend until smooth and fluffy. Scrape into a small serving bowl and top with a sprinkle of cinnamon and a drizzle of honey.

5. Serve the spring rolls with the dipping sauce.

6. The spring rolls are best served the day they are made but can be wrapped individually in plastic wrap and stored in the refrigerator for up to 1 day. The dipping sauce can be made ahead, up to 3 days in advance, and stored in an airtight container in the refrigerator.

Dates with an Orange Belt

Every date deserves an orange belt! And a little chocolate, too.

MAKES 12

- 12 Medjool dates
- 12 roasted salted almonds
- 2 navel oranges
- 1/3 cup (57 g) dark chocolate chips (vegan, if desired)
- 1/2 teaspoon coconut oil

1. Line a small rimmed sheet pan with parchment paper.

2. Carefully pry each date open. Remove the pit and replace it with an almond. Seal the date back up to enclose the almond.

3. To make the orange belts: Use a vegetable peeler to peel one long strip of orange zest around the equator of each orange. Cut each strip crosswise into thirds. Then cut each section lengthwise into 2 narrower strips about 1/4 inch thick (you should get 12 total). Trim the length of each strip so it can wrap around the middle of a date (like a belt), having the ends meet but not overlap. Put the belts aside.

4. In a small microwave-safe glass bowl, combine the chocolate chips and coconut oil. Melt in 10-second intervals, stirring each time, until melted and smooth, being careful not to overheat the chocolate. Or melt in a heat-proof glass bowl set over a pan of simmering water (don't let the bowl touch the water).

5. Dip half of each date in the melted chocolate. Wrap a belt around the chocolate-covered middle of each date. Place on the prepared pan, with the open ends of the belt down.

6. Refrigerate for about 10 minutes, or until the chocolate is set. Serve or store in an airtight container in the refrigerator for up to 1 week.

Fig and Walnut Bites

I love an "energy" ball or bite. Just a few wholesome, easy-to-find pantry ingredients, some quick pulses, and you've got a breakfast, lunch, or snack ready to go.

MAKES 14

6 dried white Turkish figs (148 g), stems removed

6 Medjool dates (132 g), pitted

3/4 cup (96 g) walnuts

1/4 teaspoon kosher salt

1/4 cup (20 g) shredded unsweetened coconut

1. In a food processor, combine the figs and dates. Pulse several times until very finely chopped. Add the walnuts and salt and pulse until the walnuts are finely chopped.

2. Pour the mixture into a bowl. For each bite, scoop out about 1 tablespoon of the mixture. Shape into a little puck or ball.

3. Put the coconut in a shallow bowl. Add the bites and coat them in coconut.

4. Store in an airtight container for up to 2 weeks.

Puffed Quinoa Chocolate Bark

Addictive. I never make enough, because these are
gone as soon as they're ready.

SERVES 4 TO 6

3 tablespoons coconut oil

2 tablespoons pure maple syrup

¼ cup (21 g) unsweetened cocoa powder

½ teaspoon pure vanilla extract

⅛ teaspoon kosher salt

1 cup (60 g) store-bought crispy puffed
quinoa

1. Line a large rimmed sheet pan with parchment paper.

2. In a medium microwave-safe bowl, combine the coconut oil and maple syrup. Heat in the microwave until the coconut oil melts. Whisk in the cocoa powder, vanilla, and salt until smooth. Add the puffed quinoa and stir until well coated.

3. Scrape the mixture onto the prepared pan and spread into an even layer about ¼ inch thick. Freeze for 20 minutes. Break into shards for serving. Store in an airtight container in the refrigerator or freezer for up to 1 week.

Strawberries with Pistachio Butter

I fell in love with pistachio butter in Italy. There is zero sugar added to ours. Just let the food processor run, and you'll end up with smooth, gooey butter to spread on toast or your favorite fruits. Strawberries are just right. You can always drizzle in a dollop of honey if you need some sweetness.

MAKES 1/2 CUP

1 cup (120 g) roasted unsalted pistachios, plus more, chopped, for serving

1 teaspoon finely grated orange zest

1 teaspoon ground cardamom (optional)

1/8 teaspoon kosher salt

1 to 2 tablespoons extra virgin olive oil

Fresh strawberries, for serving

1. In a food processor or blender, grind the pistachios for 5 to 6 minutes into a smooth paste, scraping down the sides as necessary with a silicone spatula. They will appear crumbly at first, but as they release their oils, they will turn to butter. Blend in the orange zest, cardamom (if using), and the salt. Then blend in 1 tablespoon of the olive oil until creamy. If it's still a little stiff, blend in the remaining 1 tablespoon oil.

2. Top the pistachio butter with some chopped pistachios and serve with the strawberries.

Chocolate Chia Pudding

I usually have chia pudding for breakfast, but this recipe
is fab as a dessert. Just a few easy steps, like boiling water and melting
chocolate, and you have yourself an *almost* healthful dessert.

6 SERVINGS

¼ cup (24 g) chia powder

½ cup (120 ml) water

10 Medjool dates (220 g), pitted

About 3 cups boiling water, for plumping
the dates

2 tablespoons almond butter

3 tablespoons cocoa powder, plus more
for dusting

1 teaspoon pure vanilla extract

⅛ teaspoon kosher salt

2 cups (480 ml) plant-based milk, such as
oat, almond, or cashew

¼ cup (43 g) dark chocolate chips, melted
(vegan, if desired)

1. In a small bowl, combine the chia powder and water. Let stand for about 10 minutes, stirring occasionally, until thickened.

2. Put the dates in a small mixing bowl. Add the boiling water to cover them by 1 inch and let stand for 10 minutes, or until very soft. Drain and shake out excess water.

3. In a food processor, puree the dates, almond butter, cocoa powder, vanilla, and salt. Add the milk and pulse several times to combine, then pulse in the chia mixture.

4. In a small microwave-safe glass bowl, melt the chocolate chips in 10-second intervals, stirring after each, until melted and smooth, being careful not to overheat the chocolate. (Alternatively, melt in a heat-proof glass bowl set over simmering water, being careful not to let the bowl touch the water.)

5. Scrape the melted chocolate into the food processor and pulse until well incorporated, scraping down the sides as necessary.

6. Divide the pudding among six small glasses or cups. Cover each cup tightly with plastic wrap. Refrigerate for about 4 hours, or until chilled.

7. Dust the tops with a little cocoa powder before serving.

Cherry Toast with Ricotta, Honey, and Mint

I'm not going to call this a treat. This is more of a "must." For breakfast or brunch, I love it so much, it had to be in this book.

SERVES 4

1 cup (227 g) fresh ricotta cheese

4 slices bread (gluten-free, if desired), toasted

24 fresh cherries, halved and pitted

Fresh mint leaves, for serving

Cacao nibs or block dark chocolate, for serving

Honey, for serving

1. Spread some ricotta over each piece of toast and top with cherries and mint.

2. Sprinkle with cacao nibs or, if using block chocolate, use a vegetable peeler to shave thin curls. Drizzle with a little honey.

Crispy Peanut Butter Bars

Since 1978, one of my favorite candy bars has been the Whatchamacallit. The textures and flavors thrown together make a beautiful alchemy of crisp, crunch, and sweet. This is our version, made with date syrup, found easily online or in gourmet grocers.

MAKES 16

Nonstick vegetable oil cooking spray

½ cup (128 g) smooth peanut butter

2 tablespoons date syrup

2 to 3 brown rice cakes

1 cup (170 g) dark chocolate chips (vegan, if desired)

1 teaspoon coconut oil

1. Spray an 8½ x 4½-inch metal loaf pan with cooking spray. Line the bottom and up the two long sides with parchment paper, leaving 1-inch overhangs. Line a small rimmed sheet pan with parchment paper.

2. In a medium mixing bowl, stir together the peanut butter and date syrup.

3. In another medium mixing bowl, crumble the rice cakes into very small pieces, enough to measure 1¼ cups (46 g). Stir them into the peanut butter mixture until well combined.

4. Press the mixture evenly over the bottom of the prepared loaf pan. Freeze for about 20 minutes, or until firm and sliceable. Grab the edges of the parchment and lift onto a cutting board. Cut into 8 squares, then cut the squares in half to make small bars.

5. In a small microwave-safe glass bowl, combine the chocolate chips and coconut oil. Melt in 10-second intervals, stirring each time, until melted and smooth, being careful not to overheat the chocolate. Or melt in a heat-proof glass bowl set over a pan of simmering water (don't let the bowl touch the water).

6. Using a fork, dip the bars into the chocolate to coat completely in a thin layer of chocolate, shaking off any extra. Use the edge of the bowl to scrape off the excess chocolate from the bottoms. Place on the prepared sheet pan. Refrigerate for about 20 minutes, or until the chocolate is set. Keep stored in the refrigerator for up to 2 weeks.

Espresso Tonic with Orange

Cheers to a little fizz, a touch of tart, and some fruity sweetness.

SERVES 1

1 shot (2 tablespoons) of espresso

1 teaspoon honey

½ cup (120 ml) club soda or seltzer water

1 navel orange

1 lemon

1 cinnamon stick

1. In an 8-ounce glass, stir together the espresso and honey, then add the club soda. Fill the glass with ice.

2. Using a vegetable peeler, peel off a strip of orange zest and lemon zest and add to the glass. Cut the orange in half and squeeze in some fresh orange juice. Stir with a cinnamon stick and serve.

Gluten-free · Grain-free · Vegan

Roasted Strawberry Spritz

SERVES 1

¼ cup (60 ml) Roasted Strawberries
(page 225)

1 tablespoon fresh lemon juice

6 fresh mint leaves

Club soda or seltzer water, for topping off

In an 8-ounce glass, muddle together the roasted strawberries, lemon juice, and mint. Fill the glass with ice and top off with club soda. Stir and serve.

Frozen Pops

These are perfect year-round, made easily with
ingredients you likely already have in your fridge or pantry.
Adults love them as much as kids do.

STRAWBERRY-HONEY

MAKES 6 · GLUTEN-FREE · GRAIN-FREE · DAIRY-FREE (OPTIONAL)

1¼ cups (284 g) unsweetened plain yogurt
 or plant-based yogurt

6 tablespoons (120 g) strawberry fruit spread

1 tablespoon honey

Small pinch of kosher salt

In a medium mixing bowl, stir together the yogurt, fruit spread, honey, and salt. Dividing evenly, spoon the mixture into six 3-ounce paper cups. Cover each cup with a small piece of foil. Use the tip of a paring knife to make a small slit, then slide in a Popsicle stick. Freeze for at least 3 hours, or until completely frozen. When ready to serve, remove the foil and push the pops out of the cups.

MINT CHIP

MAKES 6 · GLUTEN-FREE · GRAIN-FREE · VEGAN (OPTIONAL)

1½ cups (343 g) unsweetened plain yogurt
 or plant-based yogurt

3 tablespoons pure maple syrup

½ teaspoon pure vanilla extract

2 tablespoons cacao nibs

½ teaspoon peppermint extract

Small pinch of kosher salt

In a medium mixing bowl, stir together the yogurt, maple syrup, vanilla, cacao nibs, peppermint extract, and salt until well combined. Dividing evenly, spoon the mixture into six 3-ounce paper cups. Cover each cup with a small piece of foil. Use the tip of a paring knife to make a small slit, then slide in a Popsicle stick. Freeze for at least 3 hours, or until completely frozen. When ready to serve, remove the foil and push the pops out of the cups.

FUDGESICLE

MAKES 6 · GLUTEN-FREE · GRAIN-FREE · VEGAN (OPTIONAL)

1¼ cups (300 ml) unsweetened coconut milk, well shaken or whisked

⅓ cup (57 g) dark chocolate chips (vegan, if desired)

1 tablespoon unsweetened cocoa powder

1 tablespoon pure maple syrup

½ teaspoon pure vanilla extract

Small pinch of kosher salt

In a small saucepan, heat the coconut milk over medium heat until steaming. Add the chocolate chips, cocoa powder, maple syrup, vanilla, and salt. Whisk until the chocolate chips are completely melted. Remove from the heat and let cool to room temperature. Dividing evenly, pour the mixture into six 3-ounce paper cups. Cover each cup with a small piece of foil. Use the tip of a paring knife to make a small slit, then slide in a Popsicle stick. Freeze for at least 3 hours, or until completely frozen. When ready to serve, remove the foil and push the pops out of the cups.

CHERRY VANILLA

MAKES 6 · GLUTEN-FREE · GRAIN-FREE

1¼ cups (275 g) cottage cheese

6 tablespoons (120 g) black cherry fruit spread

¼ teaspoon pure vanilla extract

In a blender, combine the cottage cheese, fruit spread, and vanilla. Blend, scraping down the sides as necessary with a silicone spatula, until smooth and no white specks remain. Dividing evenly, spoon the mixture into six 3-ounce paper cups. Cover each cup with a small piece of foil. Use the tip of a paring knife to make a small slit, then slide in a Popsicle stick. Freeze for at least 3 hours, or until completely frozen. When ready to serve, remove the foil and push the pops out of the cups.

STRAWBERRY-
HONEY
FROZEN POP
218

CHERRY VANILLA
FROZEN POP
219

FUDGESICLE
FROZEN POP
219

MINT CHIP
FROZEN POP
218

Essential
Recipes

Oat Milk Caramel

Reducing oat milk with a little honey into a caramel was a breakthrough moment for us in our test kitchen. We could do an entire book of recipes using it. You will find it in our Peanut Crunch Cookies (page 24), Almond-Ginger Shortbread (page 36), Sticky Date Cake with Rum Caramel Sauce (page 102), and No-Churn Butter Pecan Ice Cream (page 176).

MAKES ABOUT 2/3 CUP

2 cups (480 ml) store-bought oat milk
(We use Oatly)

¼ cup (60 ml) honey

½ teaspoon pure vanilla extract

⅛ teaspoon kosher salt

In a medium high-sided saucepan, whisk together the oat milk and honey over medium-high heat. Once it comes to a boil, reduce the heat to medium so it simmers. (Keep an eye on it to make sure it doesn't boil over.) Simmer for 30 to 40 minutes, whisking occasionally, until it turns caramel color and starts to thicken. Once it has reduced to about ⅔ cup (160 ml), remove from the heat and stir in the vanilla and salt. It will continue to thicken as it cools. Use right away or keep stored in an airtight container in the refrigerator for up to 2 weeks.

Roasted Strawberries

Easy, delicious, and good to keep on hand in your fridge. We love them so much that you can find them in our Rosemary Shortcakes (page 122) and Chocolate Soufflé (page 74).

MAKES ABOUT 2 CUPS

1½ pounds (2 pints; 681 g) fresh strawberries, hulled and quartered

3 tablespoons pure maple syrup

1. Position an oven rack in the middle of the oven. Preheat the oven to 400°F.

2. In a medium, nonreactive baking dish, such as glass or ceramic, stir together the strawberries and maple syrup. Spread the strawberries in a single layer and roast for about 20 minutes, or until the strawberries soften and release their juices (this could take more or less time depending on ripeness). Let cool to room temperature, then serve, or keep stored in an airtight container in the refrigerator for up to 4 days.

Gluten-Free Pie Dough

A gluten-free pie crust can be tricky because it's delicate and may tear easily. For our beginners, you can press this recipe into the pie plate, as we do with the Banana Cream Pie (page 118). For others, it can be rolled, as in our Blueberry Galette (page 114).

MAKES ONE 10-INCH GALETTE OR 9-INCH SINGLE-CRUST PIE OR 6 SMALL GALETTES

1½ cups (222 g) gluten-free baking flour, spooned and leveled, plus more for rolling

1 tablespoon coconut sugar

½ teaspoon kosher salt

1 stick (8 tablespoons; 4 ounces; 113 g) cold unsalted butter, cut into small pieces

2 ounces (57 g) block cream cheese

2 tablespoons ice water

1. In a food processor, combine the flour, coconut sugar, and salt and pulse a few times to combine. Add the butter and cream cheese and pulse several times until crumbly. Add the water and let the processor run for about 30 seconds until large moist clumps form.

2. Pour the clumps into a large zip-top plastic bag. Use the bag to bring the dough together and shape into a ½-inch-thick smooth disk. Refrigerate for at least 30 minutes. The dough can be stored in the refrigerator for up to 2 days or frozen for up to 1 month.

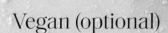

Vegan (optional)

All-Purpose Pie Dough

For those of you who prefer gluten, this is your rich, flaky, and traditional pie crust.

MAKES ONE 10-INCH GALETTE OR 9-INCH SINGLE-CRUST PIE OR 6 SMALL GALETTES

1½ cups (180 g) all-purpose flour, spooned and leveled, plus more for rolling

1 tablespoon coconut sugar

¼ teaspoon kosher salt

10 tablespoons (5 ounces; 140 g) cold unsalted butter or vegan butter, cut into small pieces

4 to 5 tablespoons ice water

1. In a food processor, combine the flour, coconut sugar, and salt. Add the butter and pulse several times in quick bursts until the butter pieces are the size of peas. (Keeping the small butter pieces intact will yield a flaky, tender crust.) Sprinkle in 4 tablespoons of the ice water. Pulse a few more times in quick bursts until small moist crumbs form and hold together when pinched. If there are some dry bits, dribble in the remaining 1 tablespoon water and pulse in. Be careful not to add too much water as it can make for a tough crust.

2. Pour the crumbs into a large zip-top plastic bag. Use the bag to bring the crumbs together and shape into a ½-inch-thick smooth disk. Refrigerate for at least 30 minutes. The dough can be stored in the refrigerator for up to 2 days or frozen for up to 1 month.

Gluten-Free Shortbread Dough

This versatile dough makes the perfect shortbread cookie,
or use it as a base for cookie bars. It is a staple.

MAKES ONE 9-INCH ROUND PAN OR
8-INCH SQUARE PAN OR 28 1½-INCH COOKIES

1 cup (148 g) gluten-free baking flour,
spooned and leveled

2 tablespoons unsweetened shredded
coconut

½ teaspoon kosher salt

½ teaspoon anise seeds (optional)

1 stick (8 tablespoons; 4 ounces; 113 g)
cold unsalted butter or vegan butter,
cut into small pieces

2 tablespoons pure maple syrup

1. In a food processor, combine the flour, coconut, salt, and anise seeds
(if using) and pulse a few times to combine. Add the butter and pulse
several times until crumbly. Add the maple syrup and let the processor run
for about 15 seconds, until large moist crumbs form.

2. If you're making the Plum Caramel Shortbread Sandwich Cookies (page
27), gather up the crumbs into a ball, then press into a ½-inch-thick smooth
disk. Wrap tightly and refrigerate for 30 minutes. If you're making the
Peanut Butter and Chocolate Bars (page 32) or Lemon Bars (page 44), go
to those recipes for press-in instructions. The dough can be stored in the
refrigerator for up to 2 days or frozen for up to 1 month.

Apricot Puree

A luxurious puree results from apricots stewed with star anise and cinnamon. We use it to fill our Apricot Rugelach (page 31), to sweeten the frosting on our Spice Cake with Whipped Apricot Frosting (page 78), and in our Apricot Custard (page 184).

MAKES ABOUT 1 CUP

8 ounces (227 g) dried apricots (about 18)

1 star anise (optional)

1 cinnamon stick (optional)

1. In a small saucepan, combine the apricots and the star anise and cinnamon stick (if using) and cover with cold water by 1 inch. Place over medium-high heat and let come to a boil, then reduce the heat to medium and simmer gently for 30 to 40 minutes, stirring occasionally, until the apricots are very soft and the liquid has nearly evaporated but still coats the bottom of the pan. Discard the star anise and cinnamon stick. Remove the pan from the heat and let cool.

2. In a food processor, puree the apricots until creamy and smooth, scraping down the sides of the bowl as necessary with a silicone spatula. Use right away or store in an airtight container in the refrigerator for up to 2 weeks or in the freezer for up to 2 months.

A WORD FROM MY DAUGHTER

Dessert means something to every household. And if it doesn't, that means something, too! It reveals how families feel about indulgence, celebration, love languages, coping, and much more.

When my mom asked me to write a guest essay for her book on desserts, my mind swirled with ideas. Having grown up in a healthy household, I didn't see dessert as a constant presence, but more as something we had for a rare occasion. It was mostly when she was working on a book that treats and desserts were readily available to try. So, early moments with dessert stand out as some of my most vivid and positive memories.

Birthday Cake

Homemade birthday cake is the best part of every birthday. Not only does it taste better, but it tastes like someone caring about you! My mom always makes perfect cakes for each of our birthdays: strawberry cake for me; chocolate peanut butter pie for my younger brother Julian; vanilla cake with chocolate frosting for my youngest brother, Shep; and carrot cake for my dad.

She decorates them with candy, flowers, and candles. They don't look store-bought, nor do they look like a frumpy pile of dough. I don't know how she does it so perfectly.

When I was about ten years old, my dad had the bold idea for my brothers and me to bake a cake from scratch for my mom's birthday. Let's just say it was a onetime occurrence. Even though the simple vanilla cake was a complete disaster (a frumpy pile of dough), we still had fun making it and the effort was appreciated. I remember sitting on the counter while my brothers each stood on a chair, watching the batter turn over on itself in the mixing bowl.

"It reveals how families feel about indulgence, celebration, love languages, coping, and much more."

Popovers

One of my favorite activities with my mom was baking popovers. I think I mostly liked saying the word "popovers," but she leaped at an activity for us to do together. She'd give me the easy tasks (like mixing things that she had already measured), and we'd eat them warm with jam when they were done.

Pancakes

Letter pancakes and "bb's" were a special breakfast, but sometimes, we would have them for dessert. My family would make pancakes together, spelling out one another's names. The *S* was always the hardest. The *J* was pretty easy and always turned out well. After a while, I got so frustrated by having an *S* first name when no one else did. With that in mind, my parents gave my youngest brother an *S* name, too, so I didn't feel left out. Quite a gesture!

"Bb's" (a term coined by my mom and her sisters when they were younger) are little pancake dots. They're made from the remnants of misshapen letters or the batter trail from the bowl to the pan. The "bb" is a symbol of the beauty in mistakes. Instead of getting upset that your letter turned out wonky, throw it in the "bb" pile of crispy little pancake dots, and suddenly it's delicious confetti.

Ice Cream

The first time I ever went somewhere alone in New York City was when I was seven years old. I went on a solo trip down the block to a local Upper West Side grocery store called Zingone Brothers. I felt like a teenager, even though I was wearing Velcro shoes and pink barrettes (actually, adults wear that now). I got there, browsed the aisles casually, and purchased a small cup of strawberry Häagen-Dazs from the cashier. It was the kind of familial place that kept cutouts of neighborhood kids and dogs on their door. They're still around today and have been for the past 100 years! After that, I'd jump at the chance to run down the block and hand-deliver my dad a pint of butter pecan or mint chip. Probably ten years later, I found out that my mom called ahead and told them I was coming. So, they pretended not to watch me and called her when I was on my way back. I'm glad I didn't know that then—it would've taken all the edge out of it.

Donuts

I was born donut-obsessed. As a kid, my principal criteria in assessing the adults in my life were "do they give me donuts?" or at least "indirect access to donuts?" At school, end-of-year class parties with donuts changed my perspective on certain teachers and the subject matter. Not only because I got to eat a donut but also because it showed me their vulnerability. I saw that they wanted their students to like them.

Like we do with New York bagels, as a hobby, our family samples and compares donuts from different shops around the city. There was a phase in our house during which there was always a box on the counter filled with glazed, hibiscus, chocolate, and cinnamon-sugar donuts. Even though they were only good for two days, those two days were ecstasy. My whole day was better knowing that the donuts were there. We'd cut them into quarters because one can only handle so much.

> "A genuine, unadulterated family moment. No curation or planning necessary. That's what dessert is to me—a salve.

Now I love donuts because they remind me of wholesome family celebrations. Donuts, and sometimes champagne, have appeared at many special occasions—before school on Valentine's Day, after Dad sold his movie to Netflix, when we each got into college, when my boyfriend asked me out for the first time, and, strangely, after my grandma Betty's funeral. I understood it as the sweetness necessary at the end of a hard day. A casual celebration of life. A genuine, unadulterated family moment. No curation or planning necessary. That's what dessert is to me—a salve. It may seem insignificant, like someone just fulfilling a craving, but those moments can bring intense connection and relief.

My mom, despite her penchant for healthy eating and living, will keep a jar of Bit-O-Honeys in her office, Charleston Chews in the freezer, and Tootsie Rolls in her bag. (She probably does not want this information out there.) There's something so adorable and tender about parents eating dessert. It's a suspension of rules and discipline to simply enjoy a moment. I've always loved seeing my parents eat dessert because it reminds me that parents aren't just parents, they're people. And sometimes they need a treat, too.

—SASCHA SEINFELD

Roasted Blueberries

I always have frozen blueberries in my freezer to use in smoothies or to make a quick dessert. Roasting them with nutmeg and maple syrup is a luscious way to top off a bowl of ice cream or yogurt. Also use them with our Date Graham Crackers (page 28) and our Sweet Oat Cake (page 70).

MAKES ABOUT 1 CUP

1 pint fresh or 10 ounces (283 g) frozen blueberries

1 teaspoon pure maple syrup

¼ teaspoon kosher salt

1 teaspoon fresh lemon juice

¼ teaspoon finely grated nutmeg

1. Position an oven rack in the middle of the oven. Preheat the oven to 375°F.

2. In a medium, nonreactive baking dish, such as glass or ceramic, stir together the blueberries, maple syrup, and salt. Roast for 15 to 20 minutes, or until the blueberries soften and start to release their juices, but still hold their shape. Let cool, then stir in the lemon juice and nutmeg. Store in an airtight container in the refrigerator for up to 4 days.

Cherry Compote

I am big on frozen fruit, especially cherries. Frozen means you can have them year-round, plus they're pitted for you. Best of all, you can make our Frozen Yogurt with Cherry Compote and Chickpea Brittle (page 164) and our incredible Chocolate Sauce (see page 134).

MAKES ABOUT 2 CUPS

3 cups (339 g) pitted fresh or frozen cherries

1 cup (151 g) seedless red grapes

¼ cup (60 ml) water

1 tablespoon brandy (optional)

Small pinch of kosher salt

1. In a small saucepan, combine the cherries, grapes, water, brandy (if using), and salt over medium heat. Once the mixture starts to boil rapidly, reduce the heat to medium so it simmers.

2. Simmer for 20 to 30 minutes, stirring occasionally, until the cherries and grapes break down and the juices reduce and start to thicken. (Break up the grapes with a spoon as they cook, if they don't break down on their own. They can be stubborn.) Let cool. Store in an airtight container in the refrigerator for up to 4 days.

Maple Whipped Cream

Most whipped creams use confectioners' sugar. We swap in maple syrup, which is still sugar, but we prefer its wholesome flavor.

MAKES 2 CUPS

1 cup (240 ml) heavy whipping cream

2 tablespoons pure maple syrup

In the bowl of a stand mixer fitted with the whisk attachment, or in a large mixing bowl with a hand mixer, beat the cream and maple syrup on medium-high speed, until soft peaks form. (Alternatively, you can whisk by hand.)

BANANA CREAM PIE   118

Acknowledgments

Sara Quessenberry: Food styling

Mark Weinberg: Photography

Mark Seliger: Cover photography

Megan Hedgpeth: Interior prop styling, art direction

Laura Palese: Book design

Anne Eastman: Prop styling assistant

Ben Weiner: Food styling assistant

Debbie Wee: Food styling assistant

Special thanks to:

Aimée Bell

Jennifer Bergstrom

Sascha Seinfeld

Ricardo Souza

INDEX

NOTE: Page references in *italics* indicate photographs.